STRESS: BIG ISSUE, BUT WHAT ARE THE PROBLEMS?

Other titles from IES:

Measuring and Monitoring Absence from Work
Seccombe I
IES Report 288, 1995. ISBN 1-85184-214-4

Employee Morale During Downsizing
Kettley P
IES Report 291, 1995. ISBN 1-85184-217-9

Leaving Employment Early
Dench S, Norton R
IES Report 322, 1996. ISBN 1-85184-250-0

Changing Roles for Senior Managers
Kettley P, Strebler M T
IES Report 327, 1997. ISBN 1-85184-255-1

Teleworking: Guidelines for Good Practice
Huws U
IES Report 329, 1997. ISBN 1-85184-257-8

Who Cares? The business benefits of carer-friendly practices
Bevan S, Kettley P, Patch A
IES Report 330, 1997. ISBN 1-85184-258-6

A catalogue of these and over 100 other titles is available from IES.

the **INSTITUTE**
for **EMPLOYMENT STUDIES**

STRESS: BIG ISSUE, BUT WHAT ARE THE PROBLEMS?

Jo Rick
Jim Hillage
Sheila Honey
Sarah Perryman

A study supported by the
IES Co-operative Research Programme

Report 331

Published by:

THE INSTITUTE FOR EMPLOYMENT STUDIES
Mantell Building
University of Sussex
Brighton BN1 9RF
UK

Tel.   + 44 (0) 1273 686751
Fax   + 44 (0) 1273 690430

Copyright © 1997 The Institute for Employment Studies

No part of this publication may be reproduced or used in any form by any means — graphic, electronic or mechanical including photocopying, recording, taping or information storage or retrieval systems — without prior permission in writing from the Institute for Employment Studies.

British Cataloguing-in-Publication Data

A catalogue record for this publication is available from the British Library

ISBN 1-85184-259-4

Printed in Great Britain by Microgen UK Ltd

The Institute for Employment Studies

The Institute for Employment Studies is an independent, apolitical, international centre of research and consultancy in human resource issues. It works closely with employers in the manufacturing, service and public sectors, government departments, agencies, professional and employee bodies, and foundations. Since it was established over 25 years ago the Institute has been a focus of knowledge and practical experience in employment and training policy, the operation of labour markets and human resource planning and development. IES is a not-for-profit organisation which has a multidisciplinary staff of over 50. IES expertise is available to all organisations through research, consultancy and publications.

IES aims to help bring about sustainable improvements in employment policy and human resource management. IES achieves this by increasing the understanding and improving the practice of key decision makers in policy bodies and employing organisations.

The IES Co-operative Research Programme

This report is the product of a study supported by the IES Co-operative Research Programme, through which a group of IES Subscribers finance, and often participate in, applied research on employment issues. The members of the CRP are:

BAA plc
Barclays Bank plc
British Broadcasting Corporation
British Steel plc
BT plc
Cabinet Office (OPS)
Department of Transport
Electricity Association
Glaxo Wellcome plc
Guardian Insurance
Halifax plc

HM Customs & Excise
Inland Revenue
Lloyds TSB Group
Marks & Spencer plc
National Westminster Bank plc
Post Office
Rolls-Royce plc
J Sainsbury plc
Shell UK Ltd
Unilever UK (Holdings) Ltd
Woolwich Building Society

Contents

Executive Summary	ix
1. Introduction	1
1.1 Background	1
1.2 The present study	1
1.3 Objectives	2
1.4 Method	2
1.5 Structure of the report	2
2. Stress — A Big Issue!	4
2.1 Current perspectives on stress	4
2.2 Stress at work in perspective	4
2.3 The changing work environment	6
2.4 Why do we use the language?	7
2.5 Occupational stress	9
2.6 Do we even speak the same language?	9
2.7 How well do models of stress reflect what goes on in organisations?	12
2.8 What does stress cost organisations?	15
2.9 Summary	17
3. Workplace Stress Management Interventions	19
3.1 Scale of intervention	19
3.2 Focus of intervention	19
3.3 Range of intervention	20
3.4 Aim of intervention	22
3.5 The evidence for intervention	24
3.6 Summary	32

4. A Framework for Intervention — 34
    4.1 Good practice — 34
    4.2 An intervention framework — 35
    4.3 Conclusion — 40

5. Conclusion and Summary — 41

Case Studies — 45
    Case Study A: Engineering Sector (large employer) — 47
    Case Study B: Financial Services Sector (large employer) — 51
    Case Study C: Marks & Spencer — 56
    Case Study D: Nationwide — 63
    Case Study E: Nestlé UK — 68
    Case Study F: The Post Office — 73
    Case Study G: Rolls-Royce, Derby — 80
    Case Study H: South West Water — 85

Bibliography — 89

Executive Summary

Occupational stress has become an everyday feature of working life. It is referred to constantly in the media and, as general understanding of the concept has grown, is used frequently to describe the way we feel about the jobs that we do. Inevitably, evidence of stress in the workplace has grown; both anecdotally and in research terms, stress is a big issue.

In fact, use of the term stress goes much further than merely expressing an emotion or feeling. Often, when we hear someone talk about stress, what we hear described is a cause and effect relationship, or someone attributing cause (often to some aspect of their work environment) for the way that they feel.

At the same time, employer responsibility (and liability) for their employees' psychological well-being is becoming ever more clearly defined. Organisations recognise the need to manage stress at work, but what is it exactly that they are trying to manage?

For all its apparent relevance to everyday life, stress is a concept beleaguered by problems of definition. It is very much an umbrella term which covers a wide range of very different aspects of work and life. There is little doubt that the work-based problems which fall under this umbrella term 'stress' can have a major impact on both individuals and the organisations for which they work. However, all too often, attention is focused on the individual, rather than recognising that the individual is an element within their environment, and examining the whole process or context of the problem. In fact, looking at stress as part of a multi-causal system facilitates good management of the situation.

Attempts to classify different types of stress management intervention have identified broad distinctions between the focus of intervention (*ie* whether interventions are targeted at the individual, team or organisational level) and the aim of intervention (*ie* whether it is to prevent stress, to react to problems in a timely way, or to heal or rectify the effects of stress). The boundaries between such levels of intervention are not always distinct, but starting to look at the targets and aims of intervention helps to underline the need for a systemic analysis of problems. It helps to focus on the specific problems that underlie general reports of stress.

Increasingly, researchers and practitioners are recognising the limitations of general, unfocused stress management initiatives and are proposing frameworks for intervention in organisations. Evidence of a strong policy on stress management was clear in all the case study organisations participating in this study. Also evident from the research literature and from the case study organisations, was the need for well designed and well evaluated interventions.

Five key elements of good practice were identified in this research:

1. **Assessment and diagnosis** — *identification of problems/concerns in the workplace. This needs to go beyond the recognition that there is anecdotal evidence of stress in the workplace. Why do organisations think they have a problem with stress (what is the evidence) and what do they mean by stress (what is the specific problem)?*

2. **Solution generation** — *what types of actions are appropriate and what are the aims in taking them? What does the organisation want to achieve in tackling the problem? What options for intervention does the organisation have? What would be the goals that the organisation hopes to achieve by intervening?*

3. **Implementation** — *if at all possible, in a way that allows for controlled comparisons. How should the intervention be structured? Over what timescale?*

4. **Evaluation** — *consequences of intervention against expectation of positive and negative outcomes. How and when will the intervention be evaluated? Are there pre-determined success criteria?*

5. **Ongoing monitoring and feedback** *into the assessment process — how can assessment findings be integrated with other management structures or policies?*

This framework for intervention includes many of the principles of good practice identified in the literature and in the practice of our case study organisations. It has the advantage of being flexible and can be adapted to many different organisational settings or problems regardless of the focus or aim of intervention. It can be used as a starting point or as a way of reviewing existing activities and identifying areas where existing interventions could be strengthened or developed.

Most importantly, this approach remains focused on the problems, and on generating and implementing realistic and achievable solutions with distinct objectives against which the impact of the intervention can be evaluated and monitored on an ongoing basis. It is this understanding, and remaining focused on specific problems that is essential. Because stress has become such a big issue in itself, and such a confused issue in terms of definition, the concept can get in the way of looking at what is actually going on in organisations and at what is, for want of a better term, good stress management practice.

1. Introduction

1.1 Background

Although today occupational stress and stress management have assumed enormous importance in organisations, stress-like phenomena have long been of concern in the world of work.

The very first academic research into what could nowadays be considered stress-like symptoms can be traced back to the early 1900s and studies into the effects of fatigue. 'Stress' first started to appear as a subject of psychological research after the Second World War. Since then, research in the area has burgeoned, and stress has moved from being the focus of academic research to assume a vast importance in our understanding and interpretation of everyday life. Inevitably, this has included the part of our lives that we spend in work.

Traditionally, it has fallen within the domain of the welfare function, and welfare officers in particular, to deal with, among other things, mental health issues in the workplace. Occupational health services often play an integral part in maintaining staff well-being. Now, stress is often regarded as a new phenomenon, often being dealt with as an issue quite independently of other health and organisational issues.

1.2 The present study

Interest in the concept of occupational stress and stress management was widespread among the major employers who form the IES Co-operative Research Programme (CRP). They funded a small study to look at research findings in the area of stress management and examples of the types of approach currently taking place in organisations. This report presents findings from the 1995/96 CRP project on stress management in the workplace.

The research critically examines our understanding of stress in the workplace. It reviews what we really know of the causes and consequences of stress, and how that in turn affects the types of interventions we choose. Ultimately, it extrapolates the principles of good practice from successful stress management interventions, and presents a more specific problem-solving framework for use in organisations.

1.3 Objectives

The objectives of the study were primarily pragmatic and focused around what constitutes good practice in occupational stress management, and what advice practitioners can take from the research findings of the academic community and from the experiences of those organisations already involved in stress management.

Specifically:

- How well do models of stress explain what goes on in organisations?
- What can organisations learn from research on stress management?

1.4 Method

There were two elements to the research: the first was broadly to summarise the results of evaluations of stress management interventions from the research literature. The size of the stress literature makes a full and comprehensive review beyond the scope of this study. Rather, the aim was to look at the main themes emerging from methodologically rigorous examinations of different approaches.

The second strand of the research was to conduct a number of case studies in organisations where stress management interventions were in operation.

1.5 Structure of the report

The report presents the findings in two sections. Chapters 2 to 3 review some of the current thinking and research literature on stress and its management. Here, the high prevalence of stress is discussed, along with its transformation from an area of social science research to a facet of apparently normal everyday experience. The current perspectives on stress and stress management are described, the evidence for the effects of stress is considered and approaches to its management summarised. Examples of good and bad stress management practice are highlighted and a process framework for intervention proposed.

Chapters 4 and 5 look at good practice that can be extrapolated from both academic research and the case studies conducted for this report.

In the second section of the report, the case studies are presented. These were all identified (mainly through the literature) as cases where methodologically sound evaluation had highlighted good practice. They represent a realistic picture of the wide range of interventions in place in organisations today.

2. Stress — A Big Issue!

2.1 Current perspectives on stress

Stress would appear to have become ubiquitous. Hardly a day goes by without some reference in the media to stress and its harmful effects. Estimates of the spiralling costs to industry are relentlessly churned out and we are warned of the 'indirect costs' about to enter the UK scene: stress-related workers compensation' (Cooper and Cartwright 1994, p.65). As Newton (1995) notes of the current *status quo* in the introduction to his alternative analysis of stress:

> 'Wherever you turn there are a multiplicity of guides on the nature of stress . . . . In academic texts or in popular media articles we learn how stress is a fact of our modern busy lives and how we should watch for the danger signs of stress.'

Since the war, we have seen stress undergo a complete transformation from a subject of academic research to a concept synonymous with modern living. Haward (1960), points out that before the war, 'stress' was virtually unknown outside engineering. Whereas in the five years prior to 1940 no papers using this term were listed in psychological research abstracts, by 1960, a comprehensive review of stress publications covered over 25,000 papers. In the 36 years since then, this exponential trend in stress publications has not stopped. The literature relating to occupational stress (both academic and lay) continues to be one of the fastest growing. Apparently, we face a blight on modern living of epidemic proportions. But is this really the case?

2.2 Stress at work in perspective: popular beliefs and the measurement of stress

Are we really being confronted by an explosion in stress levels? Through the 1980s and 1990s, media articles have warned of the increase of stress in the workplace. At the same time, there has been a small, but consistent, questioning by researchers as to whether such an increase has actually taken place. Without doubt, we have witnessed a massive increase in general awareness of stress, but has this been matched by an increase in the experiences that we now call stress?

Newton (1995) argues that we actually cannot know if stress levels have risen, even if surveys do indicate increasing stress. This is because what Newton refers to as the 'discourse' about stress, (*ie* popular beliefs about stress, and the words and language that we use to describe and group our experiences under the heading 'stress') has been growing at the same time. As Newton argues:

> *'The ability to express stress depends on the ability to learn the language of stress and the parameters of the stress discourse. . . . By the same token, apparent increases in stress surveys, say conducted between 1944 and 1994, may simply reflect the increasing post war spread of the discourse.'* (p.10).

In other words, the more commonly understood the term becomes, the greater the usage and application will be, and inevitably the number of people who can identify their experiences as stress will increase. Clear comparisons can be drawn with growing recognition of other 'modern' complaints such as Repetitive Strain Injury (RSI) and Chronic Fatigue Syndrome (CFS). Both these conditions have only comparatively recently been recognised, although the symptoms and the experience of these conditions existed prior to the condition having a name. To some extent, any apparent increase in levels of RSI or CFS, for example, may reflect an increased recognition of the condition rather than an increase in the experience of the symptoms of that condition.

Without a doubt, the overall numbers of reports of work-based stress are increasing, but that in itself does not help us to understand or explain what happens to individuals in organisations. We need to know *why* such reports are on the increase and *what* such reports of stress actually mean in individual and organisational terms.

2.3 The changing work environment

Other changes have been occurring in the workplace. In general terms, Health and Safety legislation has actually improved working conditions. Nowadays, work environments are far less harmful to our physical health. As a result, mental health issues have been brought to the fore, and in recent years, legislation has clearly identified mental health as a responsibility of employers.

In their practical occupational health guide for managers, Fingret and Smith (1995) identified another reason which might contribute to this apparent 'increase' in stress. As work has become far less physical, the psychological health of employees has assumed more importance. One conclusion it is possible to draw is that this increased salience does not necessarily mean that levels of psychological health have changed, simply that they have become more visible facets of work and performance.

This increased concern with mental health issues in relation to work can be seen in the way that we think about and collect information on people's experience of work. Official surveys of work experience such as, for example, the *Labour Force Survey* now include questions which allow the impact of mental health problems on work performance to be more specifically identified. The inclusion of such questions indicates the way in which, in general, accounts of self reported levels of psychological symptoms are increasing. This means that we see more evidence of work stress because it is now being measured.

There is no way of telling whether experienced stress levels, as opposed to awareness and measurement of stress, have genuinely risen over the last few decades. What is certain is that stress became a very big issue in the 1980s, grew in importance in the 1990s and looks set to stay that way in the next millennium.

> The implications for those working in organisations are significant. We are very likely to hear far higher levels of anecdotal evidence of work stress, but what that means for the organisation, or for the individuals employed there, is not clear.

2.4 Why do we use the language?

If increased awareness of the idea of stress does not necessarily reflect increased experience of stress why has the concept been taken on in such a wholesale way? If it does not describe what is happening to us, why are we so concerned about it and why do we use the idea so much?

The concept of stress is unique in its appeal to both academic and general public audiences. It is difficult to identify any other single social science research area which has achieved such a high profile over so many years as that of stress and, in particular, stress at work. There are many reasons why this might be the case, but two in particular have been suggested which could help to explain the wholesale adoption of stress as a construct of everyday life: firstly, its saliency and secondly, its empowering of individuals. Both these ideas are discussed next.

2.4.1 Its immediate and widespread saliency

Stress is appealing

The stress concept has high face value. It appeals in common sense terms and provides a simple but all encompassing analysis of any source of distress in everyday life. The stress language enables us to explain our experiences in scientific and therefore valid ways. Simply the fact that stress has been taken on board in such a wholesale way and is now firmly rooted in everyday usage gives weight to the apparent value of the concept. Something that is so universally accepted and intuitively sensible must be right.

Some research in 1988 looked at the way people talk about stress and ill health. Pollock (1988) identified the way in which people use stress to explain anything from everyday ailments to serious medical conditions. In discussing the concept of stress, Pollock points to what is possibly the most alluring aspect:

> 'its capacity to provide an explanation for illness that goes beyond the sheer arbitrariness of random events.'

Stress is appealing because it allows us to interpret and explain some of the things that happen to us in everyday life. It reduces uncertainty, and consequently it appears to give us more control over some of the negative aspects of our lives.

2.4.2 Its apparent empowering of the individual

Stress is empowering

The concepts of stress, and particularly of stress management, are seductive because they allow us to feel that we understand and are in control of what happens to us. The attraction lies in the way that stress allows us to understand our feelings and experiences in scientific terms, and importantly, it allows us to prescribe cause and effect, rather than face uncertainty about why we feel the way that we do.

Pollock argues that the proliferation of research into stress, the claims made about its effects, and its assumed causal link to illness have created a modern myth.

> 'Stress is a manufactured concept which has by now become a 'social fact'. As such, it has direct implications for the ways people see their world and act within it.' (Pollock, 1988)

If we can understand and explain why we feel the way we do, then we are in a much better position to change either what is causing the problem or (as is far more often the case) change the way we feel about it, or our reaction to it. The wide range of self help and stress management guides currently available support the idea that by analysing our stress we are in a better position to act and reduce the negative consequences for ourselves.

> Identifying stress puts us in control, because once we know what is wrong we can act to change things for the better.

These are two highly persuasive reasons for individuals. Here is a scientific concept that can readily be applied to everyday life, to explain and attribute cause for our experiences and which, at the same time, apparently helps us to take control of things and make them better. However, this apparent empowerment also carries with it a responsibility for action. Once cause and effect have been established, the impetus is on resolving or managing either the source, or more commonly, the uncomfortable feelings caused by the stress.

> When an individual talks about stress, we hear them not only expressing a feeling or experience, but often describing a cause and effect relationship, or attributing cause for the way they feel.

2.5 Occupational stress

There are also a number of reasons why stress has become an issue for organisations. Two of the most commonly stated are that:

- work stress has been demonstrated to cause a range of individual symptoms, which can affect people's performance at work
- work stress is linked to adverse organisational outcomes, and consequently to lower productivity and organisational inefficiency.

Stress is a well established concept in our everyday life. Legislation and change in working practices have resulted in mental health issues gaining more prominence in the workplace. At the same time, stress has provided an easily understood and readily applied explanation of why we feel the way we do, and enables us to apparently take control and reduce the negative consequences of our experiences. Organisations have also reacted to fears about stress, motivated by concern for employee well-being, and fears about the adverse consequences for their organisation of lower productivity and high absence levels.

So, stress is undoubtedly a big issue. But how well does it help us to understand what happens to people in organisations? Are researchers and the general public talking about the same thing? How well do models of stress help us to understand and resolve organisational problems?

2.6 Do we even speak the same language?

This brings us to one of the central aims of this research. Do the models of stress that appear in the literature explain how aspects of work affect individuals, and lead to illness and inefficiency? To what extent do academic perspectives match lay perspectives?

2.6.1 General use of stress

So far, this report has used 'stress' in its broadest sense, in the way that it is used every day without trying to define exactly what it means. One of the key questions here is what people are talking about when they refer to stress. In fact, the word 'stress' has a variety of different uses and meanings.

It is common to hear the view that there is positive stress and negative stress, and that it is only the negative stress that is bad for you — where 'stress' means an external challenge or pressure to perform. It is also very common to hear people say they 'have stress' or 'feel stressed', when stress refers to the uncomfortable internal reaction to an experience or situation. Often, people describe work as stressful, or identify a particular aspect of their job, or working with a particular colleague, as stressful. In this case, the stress might be the job you do, or a part of it, or a difficult personal relationship. We also use stress to describe other emotional states, such as anger, frustration, boredom, depression or anxiety. We also use stress in a medical way, to explain anything from headaches to cardiovascular heart disease, as well as organisational outcomes, such as inefficiency or absenteeism.

> In lay terms, stress is used on a daily basis to mean almost anything. Everyone will have their own understanding of the word, but it becomes very confusing and very difficult to understand what a person means when they say that they are stressed or that something is stressful. General consensus is that stress is something we suffer from, but what it is exactly remains very unclear.

2.6.2 Research definitions of stress

Even within a research setting, there is no consensus on a definition of stress. A variety of models exist, all of which purport to demonstrate the relationship between work, stress, and individual and organisational outcomes, but all with their own problems. Reviewers such as Ivancevich *et al.* (1990), have pointed to the 'modest agreement' that exists around what stress involves. But that agreement rests on the elements that exist in models of stress, not on how those elements interact with each other to cause stress and ill health.

Research definitions generally agree that 'stress' is an umbrella term or organising concept, comprising a number of different elements. Distinguishing between these elements helps us to clarify and understand what stress is, and what it is describing in individual and organisational terms.

There are three main areas to consider here:

- **Stressors**, *ie* the things people report as causing them to be stressed (*eg* workload)

- **Strain**, *ie* the symptoms reported as a result of experiencing stressors (*eg* irritability, anxiety, raised blood pressure)

- **Stress outcomes**, *ie* the presumed consequences of strain (*eg* past performance, increased absence, increased accidents).

Perhaps the most helpful way for organisations to think about stress as an issue is as a rubric or general heading. This approach was first suggested by Lazarus in 1966, who advocated the use of the word 'stress' as an organising concept. Lazarus and Folkman (1984) reaffirm their opinion that this is the most useful approach within a sphere of meaning in which they propose psychological stress as:

> '. . . the particular relationship between the person and the environment that is appraised by the person as taxing or exceeding their resources and endangering their well-being.'

Within such a sphere of reference the onus is on researchers to identify and measure the antecedents, processes and outcomes. In other words, the word stress can refer to a wide range of processes that link stressors with strain and stress outcomes. Within this, however, Lazarus and Folkman emphasise that stress is part of a multi-causal system. Other conditions must also be present to cause stress-related disease and that research must focus some attention on the contributions of these other variables and processes as mediators of the stress-illness relationship.

In organisational terms, it makes very little sense to look only at stress outcomes or levels of strain without looking at individuals within their environments, and looking at the whole process or context of the problem.

The idea of stress as part of a multi-causal system is an important one. Only a systemic analysis can identify the reasons for any reported problems. Stress as an explanation is only useful when the individual is being looked at and concentrated on as part of the organisational system.

2.7 How well do models of stress reflect what goes on in organisations?

Because stress is related to individual perceptions and desires, it can relate to many different things. One model of stress which attempts to conceptualise this in work terms is that proposed by Cooper and Marshall (1976), who suggest that there are six sources of stressful events at work (Figure 2:1). These are indicated on the left hand side of the model. It is important to avoid thinking of these areas as 'objective stressors'. Rather, they are a way of categorising the different areas where problems can arise. Whether or not stress will lead to the strain symptoms and diseases (listed on the right) depends not simply on the amount of stress or the length of exposure, but also on the individual's ability to influence or cope with the situation in which they find themselves.

This leads to the second problem with whether or not models describe individual experiences in work. Although they clearly suggest links between individual negative experiences (stressors and strain), they do not explain how stress causes strain, or the stress outcomes such as reduced organisational efficiency (indicated on the right hand side of the model in Figure 2:1).

2.7.1 Stress, strain and stress outcomes

Much of the research on stress is carried out using self-completion questionnaires. The format is usually to ask individuals a range of questions about the nature of their work and the type of job they do; about relationships with managers, colleagues, clients or customers; about their role, their level of autonomy, role clarity, workload, interest in the job, promotion or career opportunities; about feedback and communications where they work, and the organisational structure and climate. Because most of the research is based on self report (self-completion questionnaires), most of our knowledge about the consequences is focused on individual outcomes.

Stress is associated with a range of negative consequences for individuals, such as reduced job satisfaction, lower organisational commitment, depression, anxiety, poor job performance and ill health. The relationship between stress and strain is often far more complex that that suggested in models of stress. Given the wide array of potential stressors, the fact that

Figure 2:1 Model of the dynamics of work stress

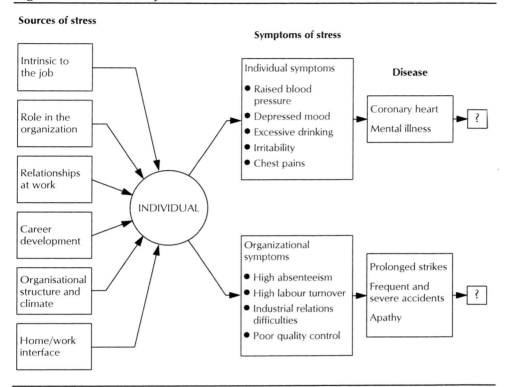

Source: HSE (adapted from Cooper and Marshall, 1976)

individuals have different resources and responses to the same situation or demand, and that strain can mean the reporting of anything from minor to very severe symptoms, it becomes clear that 'stress' can mean a great number of different things.

As a result, research findings on stress can appear inconclusive, or even conflicting. Take, for example, the relationship between stress and ill health. The idea that stress helps to explain disease is firmly established in popular thought. Pollock, in a 1988 study where she interviewed 114 adults on their ideas about the nature of health and illness, found that stress was a dominant theme in explaining ill health. This was particularly the case when explaining nervous breakdowns or heart attacks (as opposed to cancer), but was also commonly cited as the cause of everyday symptoms, such as severe headaches or stomach pains. This association between stress and ill health is commonly accepted by most of the research community as well.

In recent years, much research has focused more specifically on the effects of work-based stress on psychological and physical well-being. There is a wealth of evidence to suggest that stress can have an adverse effect on the quality of life. Recent research has linked stress with neuroses, coronary heart disease and other conditions, such as dyspepsia and ulcers (Pearlin, Lieberman, Menaghan and Mullan, 1981; Jenner, 1986). It has also been suggested that experiencing feelings of stress is an important factor in a range of other complaints (Cox, 1985). Stress can affect not only an individual's health but also their performance and interpersonal relationships (Stewart, 1987). In a work environment, the result of exposure to short or long-term stressors will affect a person's ability to perform well and their relationships with their colleagues (Stewart, 1987). Often, work-based stress can affect an individual's quality of life away from the job (Dooley, Rook and Catalano, 1987; Warr, 1987).

However, there is still debate about the nature of the stress-health link. Fingret and Smith conclude that:

> *'A continual or recurrent state of stress can eventually lead to anxiety states and depression. Stress has also been shown to be associated with diseases such as cancer and coronary heart disease. Not all mental ill health rises from a gradual deterioration of mental well-being. Although there is disagreement about the influence of the environment on the development of some forms of mental illness such as depression and schizophrenia, in many individuals, these diseases [schizophrenia and depression] seem to arise without any reference to the general psychosocial environment.'*

Reynolds and Shapiro (1991), in an overall review of stress management, also find that 'the strength of the relationship between stress and illness is controversial, and typically, environmental stressors such as life events or daily hassles, are found to account for only a small amount of variance in illness'. In other words, although links can be demonstrated between stress and ill-health, their findings suggest that among other factors, stress has only a marginal impact on health.

The causal link between stress and ill health is widely accepted both by the general public and by researchers, and is implicit in many of the models that exist of occupational stress. In fact, the research on stress and ill health shows a far more complex picture to that presented in most models. More importantly, stress models often imply a causal relationship with ill health independently of other risk factors. Mackay and Cooper (1987) point out that psychosocial factors cannot be viewed in isolation from more reliably established risk factors.

The debate that centres around the extent to which stress causes ill health can also be found in relation to other individual consequences (job satisfaction, poor performance, depression) and in relation to stress outcomes (absenteeism, inefficiency, prolonged strikes). Part of the problem here is that when we try to assess the extent to which stress is a cause of any form of strain or stress outcome, we tend to look at the individual (usually based on their own self report) in isolation from their working environment, rather than recognising that they are an element within the organisational system.

This means that we tend to assume that high workload, for example, is an objective stressor, independent of any organisational context, whereas in fact, what 'high workload' means will vary enormously for different people in different jobs, or for similar jobs in different organisations. The way in which it affects an individual may well depend on organisational factors (for example, consequences of missed deadlines). The only way to really understand what is happening to people in organisations is to look at the system as a whole.

2.8 What does stress cost organisations?

We use stress as shorthand to refer to what are a lot of very different stressors, strains and stress outcomes. We tend to see it as a process that affects individuals, although the links between stressors, strain and stress outcomes is not always clear. This means that although we use stress to describe how we feel, or we identify 'stress' as the problem, it does not really tell us anything about what happens to individuals in organisations. In some ways, it is more helpful to think of stress as an attribution (for example: 'my workload is causing my stress') rather than an explanation, which is likely to be more complex.

Many attempts to calculate the costs of stress use absence data based on combinations of 'stress, anxiety and depression', or 'stress and other mental illness', as well as statistics from other disease groups, such as cardiovascular heart disease. Part of the reason that stress has become such a big issue, requiring immediate attention, is because of its apparent cost to industry.

Some of the statistics are drawn from sources which use self-reported stress. As shown earlier in this chapter, the way 'stress' is used can vary enormously, and it is sometimes difficult to know exactly what is included, in broad estimates, as to the costs of stress. As a result, such estimates as to the costs of stress vary enormously. Some examples of these discrepancies are given below:

- Cox (1993, p.60), in a report commissioned by HSE, reports on Department of Health, and Department of Social Security figures. He points out that the data are imprecise for a number of reasons, and that it is impossible to extrapolate trend data due to changes in recording systems. As a result, such figures are only useful for an educated guess. Cox goes on to highlight other research that has suggested 40 million working days are lost annually due to 'stress related disorders', and that up to 60 per cent of all work absence is caused by 'stress related disorders'.
- Cooper, writing in 1994, reports that the Confederation of British Industry (CBI) figures calculate 360 million days lost annually at a cost of £8 billion, and that the Health and Safety Executive (HSE) estimate *at least* half of these lost days relate to 'stress related absence'.
- Fingret and Smith (1995, p.60) calculate that 80 million days are lost through all forms of 'stress related and mental illness'. Working again from CBI and Department of Health data, employers estimated that 30 per cent of sickness absence was related to 'stress, anxiety and depression'.

The only thing that can really be concluded from such divergent estimates of the costs of stress is that we currently do not have the accounting systems in place to make any realistic assertions about the cost impact of mental health or other diseases on British industry, let alone the proportion of those costs which may be due to stress. These figures, on the national costs of stress, do contribute to making stress a big issue, but do not help employers in understanding the scale of the problems that might exist in their organisations.

> The best advice for organisations is to look closely at their own ways of recording sickness absence, and conduct their own analysis as to the type and size of problems that exist in their workforce.

2.9 Summary

We have witnessed an unprecedented growth in stress awareness over the last few decades. For individuals and organisations alike, the concept of stress is a seductive one, combining both explanation and control.

It is unsurprising, given its high level of exposure in the media, and its versatility in describing a wide array of feelings, symptoms and situations, that nowadays stress is viewed by many as an ever increasing problem which needs to be tackled urgently. It is perceived by many of us as something to be blamed for all our ills, and accepted by many as a natural condition of our working and personal lives. Furthermore, the causal link between stress and ill health is widely accepted.

Models of stress list many facets of working life which can be sources of stress. As such, stress can be seen as an umbrella term, or a grouping concept. This versatility in part explains why stress is such a big issue now. Far from describing a single process, stress is often identified as the cause of a wide range of personal and organisational ills. It is only by going beyond the general organising concept that employers can identify specific problems in their organisations, understand the dynamics, and attempt to implement solutions. But, to achieve this, stress has to be seen as part of a multi-causal system. Stress is useful as an explanation only when an individual is being considered as part of the organisational system.

A closer look at the research demonstrates how two of the very factors that have helped to make stress such an easily accessible concept (and as a result, such a big issue) are actually shown to be far more complex issues in the academic research literature on stress:

- Stress research has played an important role in bringing attention to the issue of psychological well-being and how it can be affected by the workplace. However, the research findings also demonstrate that these are complex sets of inter-relations at work, and understanding what happens to individuals in organisations is often not as simple or clear cut as is sometimes assumed from models of occupational stress.
- Consequently, we cannot know on a wide scale the extent to which stress affects organisations, or its cost to industry. Although research so far has helped point the way, organisations

need to focus on individuals in the context of their own organisational environment and systems if they are to gain a full understanding of any problems that exist in the workplace.

The next chapter goes on to examine our understanding of stress management, to look at some of the more successful stress management interventions, and to extrapolate the factors that appear to influence success in dealing with organisational problems.

3. Workplace Stress Management Interventions

3.1 Scale of intervention

As concern about the impact of stress on individual and organisational performance has grown, so has the amount of information available on how to manage stress, and the number and variety of stress management programmes. Palmer and Dryden, in their 1994 review of approaches and interventions, note the near exponential increase in the publication of research papers in this field of work. The management of stress is now well established far beyond academic circles. Cooper and Cartwright (1994) describe the current prevalence of stress management programmes thus:

> 'In the last few years there has been an explosion of health promotion or 'wellness' programmes in US and UK industry. Such activities as exercise, stress management training, smoking cessation and counselling are being encouraged by virtually every medium available — radio, TV, magazines, books — and are taking place not only in the home, schools, etc. but also in the workplace.'

3.2 Focus of intervention

As discussed in the previous chapter, much of the research on stress has collected data on a self-report basis, and has inevitably led to an almost exclusive focus on the individual outcomes resulting from stress. In line with this, the focus of much research on coping and stress management has been to examine the ways in which individuals can cope with stress (Ivancevich et al., 1990).

The result is that there is extensive advice on individual stress management techniques. This has been true both in the popular conception of stress and in the academic research. Newton describes this as the constant urging in both media and academic literature to:

> 'Watch out for the "danger signs" of stress . . . monitor our "stress levels", analyse our "coping strategies", and learn how to become "stress fit" through a range of "stress management techniques".'

Articles on individual techniques for stress management appear regularly in the media, and a wide range of self help books on this subject are available. It is arguably in part due to the level of stress management information readily available which contributes to the appeal of the stress concept. Models of stress supply us with a way of interpreting and attributing cause to a wide range of (usually negative) experiences and emotions. At the same time, the many sources of advice on how to deal with stress promote the idea of individual empowerment, and suggest that we can take control of, and resolve, stressful situations.

In fact, this focus on reducing individual symptoms of stress in no way reflects the range of different activities that researchers think might help to reduce stress in the workplace. The next section goes on to look at the different targets and the different objectives associated with types of intervention.

3.3 Range of intervention

By the late 1980s, reviews of the literature identified a broad range of interventions which were being studied for their efficacy in managing stress. These included interventions which were aimed not only at changing the individual, but changing their relationship with the organisation, or the organisation itself.

Table 3:1 offers one way of summarising levels of stress management intervention and associated outcomes. It is reproduced from DeFrank and Cooper's 1987 review of worksite stress management interventions. It should be pointed out that this is a theoretical framework. That is to say, that the interventions at each level (on the left of the table) can, in theory, result in one or several of the outcomes (on the right of the table).

At the individual intervention level, DeFrank and Cooper list techniques which concentrate on the individual person and deal

Table 3:1 Levels of stress management interventions and outcomes

Interventions	Outcomes
Focus on individual	**Focus on individual**
Relaxation techniques	Mood states (depression, anxiety)
Cognitive coping strategies	Psychosomatic complaints
Bio-feedback	Subjectively experienced stress
Meditation	Physiological parameters (blood pressure)
Exercise	Sleep disturbances
Employee assistance programmes	Life satisfaction
Time management	
Focus on individual/organisational interface	**Focus on individual/organisational interface**
Relationships at work	Job stress
Person-environment fit	Job satisfaction
Role issues	Burnout
Participation and autonomy	Productivity and performance
	Absenteeism
	Turnover
	Healthcare utilisation and claims
Focus on organisation	**Focus on organisation**
Organisational structure	Productivity
Selection and placement	Turnover
Training	Absenteeism
Physical/environmental job characteristics	Healthcare claims
Health concerns and resources	Recruitment/retention success
Job rotation	

Source: DeFrank and Cooper, 1987

with the ways in which he or she responds to problems regardless of the source of that problem.

The next level emphasises the interface between individuals and organisations. DeFrank and Cooper list a range of potential outcomes at this level which are both subjective (*eg* perspectives on job satisfaction) and objective (absenteeism and turnover).

The third level identifies the organisation as the target for intervention. Here, the emphasis is on changing what are believed to be environmental sources of stress within the organisation. Organisational outcomes as a result of stress management intervention are also listed.

DeFrank and Cooper also identify the overlap between the different levels of intervention.

> 'It should be noted that there is a degree of unavoidable overlap in this ordering, as the levels are not independent of each other.

> *For example, the impact of the physical characteristics of the job will be modified to some extent by the individual's perception of them. On the other hand, the availability of time to meditate may be a function of environmental demands.'*

In other words, this type of classification highlights the need for a systemic analysis of the problems in organisations which looks at the individual within their organisational context. It is misleading to focus on the individual alone and exclude the role of environmental influences. In fact, a systemic analysis (for example, that examines the processes and systems within which an individual is operating) helps to make sense of the levels of intervention proposed by DeFrank and Cooper because it helps to shift the focus onto specific problems rather than general 'stress'. Intervention at the individual level assumes that analysis has pinpointed the problem to the individual's *responses* to their situation. Intervention at a structural level, for example, doesn't necessarily imply that it is the structure that is causing individual 'stress'. Rather, that the cause of the organisation's problem is structural, and therefore a structural solution is appropriate.

Bearing this in mind, the categories presented in Table 3:1 play an extremely useful role in helping to understand the broad context of stress management in two very different but key ways:

- first, in understanding what organisations are aiming to achieve by introducing stress management interventions
- second, in understanding the research on stress management.

Each of these are dealt with in turn below.

3.4 Aim of intervention

Looking at stress management in the way it is represented in Table 3:1 inevitably raises questions about what organisations want to achieve by introducing an intervention. What are the goals or objectives of intervention and are they clear?

As discussed in Chapter 2, stress can mean a large variety of different things and can be used to describe quite diverse problems or feelings. From Table 3:1 it can be seen that the term 'stress management' refers to a range of activities that can have very different foci and outcomes.

Table 3:2 Aims of intervention

	Individual	Organisational
Primary	To reduce the risk factor or change the nature of the stressor	To remove the hazard or reduce employees' exposure or its impact on them
Secondary	To alter the ways in which individuals respond to the risks and stressors	To improve the organisation's ability to recognise and deal with stress related problems as they arise
Tertiary	To heal those who have been traumatised or distressed at work	To help employees cope with and recover from problems at work

Source: Cox, 1993

A helpful way to think about what different stress management interventions are trying to achieve is given by Cox (1993). He identifies three broad aims of intervention (see Table 3:2) and illustrates the way they can be characterised at individual and organisational levels.

Primary interventions are concerned with the prevention of stress in the workplace, typically through risk assessment and hazard control, or through generalised stress management training.

Secondary interventions can be characterised as 'timely reaction', where organisations or individuals are alert to or monitor for potential problems. This, in turn, facilitates recognising dangers and responding appropriately to resolve problems or relieve situations as they arise and so minimise the impact.

Tertiary interventions are to do with curing the effects of stress. They are aimed at helping people to recover once they are suffering the ill effects of stress.

All too often, stress management interventions are brought into an organisation in response to general concerns about stress levels, without any analysis of specific problems and identification of appropriate strategies. But the likelihood of interventions being successful is greatly enhanced if they are clearly targeted at resolving specific problems rather than if they are assumed to have some positive effect in a very general, non-specific way. Once again, the need for a systemic analysis is underlined.

> What clearly emerges from all this is that just as 'occupational stress' covers a multitude of work factors, so 'stress management' refers to a diverse array of techniques and activities with different targets and different objectives.
>
> It becomes essential for organisations to have a very clear understanding of the nature of the specific problems with which they are concerned if they hope to implement appropriate solutions, with clear targets and objectives.

We can now review what evidence there is in support of stress management intervention from the research literature.

3.5 The evidence for intervention

Sadly, good quality evaluations of stress management interventions are relatively sparse. In addition, stress management interventions are diverse and, as a result, research findings can be difficult to compare. In order to provide organisations with advice about the types of outcomes associated with different interventions, it is only really feasible to compare like with like.

We have chosen to focus on two types of intervention in this review. The first, counselling (individual level), because it is becoming an ever more common response to occupational stress, often as part of an Employee Assistance Programme (EAP). The second, job redesign, because the indications from the research literature are that this is seen as the way forward for stress management, and the conclusions of researchers who have reviewed the literature seem largely favourable in terms of what organisational level interventions could have to offer in the future.

The intention here is to examine each approach in turn, and:

- give examples of the findings from methodologically robust studies
- identify the processes underlying the intervention that appear to contribute to success
- identify any points of caution raised in the literature.

3.5.1 Counselling interventions

Much of the evidence in its support of counselling comes from general settings, although there is a growing body of work that looks at the effectiveness of worksite counselling. Generally speaking, such studies demonstrate that those who seek and receive counselling are psychologically better off as a result than those who seek but do not receive counselling. Most reviewers conclude that there is promising evidence for worksite counselling. This section looks at some of the findings associated with four such evaluations.

Firth-Cozens and Hardy (1992) looked at data from 90 white collar workers suffering from stress at work who were clinically depressed. All clients were referred for counselling by their GPs specifically for psychological distress associated with their jobs. The counselling in this instance took the form of psychotherapy and was more intense and prolonged than most worksite counselling. Self report assessments taken at the referral stage and at 16 weeks, showed significant improvements on a range of standard outcome measures as a result of counselling. These measures included general psychological functioning, self-esteem, aspects of work, job characteristics and job satisfaction. The only measure not to show a change was perceived variety in job. Large positive changes were found in perceived opportunity for control, feelings of competency, the effects of work on home life and intrinsic satisfaction in the job. Firth-Cozens and Hardy suggest that as symptom levels are reduced, so perceptions of jobs become more positive. However, as they go on to point out, this does not mean that symptoms cause job perceptions or *vice versa*. They conclude that individual factors, such as stress symptoms, are clearly related to the ways in which people see their job. Nevertheless, the results also suggest that job conditions still play a role.

It is important to note the role of assessment problem diagnosis in this example. GPs referred clients following diagnosis of clinical depression and psychological distress *associated with their jobs*. Hence, it was realistic to evaluate the counselling in terms of the impact it had on perceptions of work. The role of evaluation was also crucial, not just in terms of client satisfaction with the service, but in demonstrating the ways in which counselling can impact on perceptions of work. Whether the results of this intervention had an impact on more behavioural outcomes such as absenteeism is impossible to say, as this was not the primary focus of the research and such measures were not included in the evaluation.

Other studies of counselling have used more objective measures such as absenteeism to assess the impact of counselling in an organisational setting.

3.5.2 Worksite counselling

The Post Office counselling service is one of the best known and best researched. It was set up in response to concern about objective evidence that mental health and psychological problems were the second largest cause of early retirement after muscular-skeletal illness. Evaluation showed that the largest cluster of problems reported by people coming for counselling could be broadly identified as mental health and stress issues (46 per cent) followed by relationship problems (24 per cent). Those who underwent counselling showed great improvements in both mental health and reduced sickness absence. However, their mental health and absence levels remained worse after counselling than did those of the control group and there were not comparable improvements in other outcome measures, such as job satisfaction and organisational commitment (Cooper & Cartwright, 1994).

Again, this study illustrates how problem diagnosis (in this case the early retirement data) plays an essential role in identifying both problems and appropriate solutions. In this example, evaluation was more work focused and researchers found a significant decrease in levels of absenteeism as a result of going to counselling.

A final example of counselling as an intervention to manage stress is provided by Highly and Cooper (1996). Their research compared results from counselling across nine organisations and found that after counselling, clients reported improvements in work-related mental well-being and physical well-being. However, they found no change in either job satisfaction or sources of pressure scales.

Highly and Cooper argue that this is not surprising, given that counselling is aimed at helping people cope with their personal and work lives better. Counselling is not an organisational level intervention and therefore organisational issues such as sources of pressure and job satisfaction (with various aspects of their job) are unlikely to be affected. Highly and Cooper's study provides broadly positive results in specific areas. Methodologically speaking, their study looked at several organisations which already had counselling services in operation. They also found that there were differences in results across organisations. This implies that it is not simply having a counselling service, but the way that an organisation implements and integrates it into organisational processes that will affect the relative success of such an intervention. In other words, Highly and Cooper were looking at counselling in general as a response to stress, whereas the previous studies were looking at counselling as an intervention to deal with a specific and well-defined problem.

Again, this underlines the need for organisations to undertake systemic analyses to identify problems. This in turn allows targeted interventions with realistic objectives against which outcomes can be measured.

Highly and Cooper go on to conclude that companies need to look very closely at why they want counselling services and what they hope to achieve. Overall, counselling can be effective in helping individuals, but does not necessarily have an impact measurable at the organisational level.

3.5.3 Other issues for counselling in an organisational setting

Identifying objectives for stress management interventions is only part of the process. A further consideration for organisations is ensuring that any intervention is evaluated carefully against its goals. A recent study demonstrates just how valuable such evaluation can be.

McKay, King, Slawek and Wedderburn (1996) reported on an intervention to counsel industrial shift workers about health concerns. Their research design used a very sophisticated and robust methodology. Workers self selected to take part in the process, and initial assessment showed that the majority of individuals had sleeping or eating problems. In fact, 98 per cent of participants reported sleeping problems (over 70 per cent of which were associated with working night shifts) and 83 per cent of participants reported eating problems (again, 70 per cent of these were associated with working night shifts). The counselling intervention was a 'brief' therapy found to be highly successful in other similar situations and involved an initial consultation with two follow-up sessions.

Measurements were taken pre- and post-intervention on a number of indicators. Satisfaction with the intervention among participants was very high, with 92 per cent saying that they would recommend it to a colleague, and 75 per cent saying they thought they would stick to the changes that they had made as a result of the brief therapy. Other positive ratings were made on features of the intervention such as: 'listening', 'making sense', 'reassuring', and 'understanding'. However, the researchers found very little evidence of any change on outcome measures relating to mental health and well-being and physiological symptoms, although the trends were all positive.

One outcome of the research is to highlight the essential role of evaluation in assessing whether or not interventions are successful in achieving their objectives. In this example, workers indicated a high level of satisfaction with the service. Had that been the only outcome measure and the intervention continued, it could have created a system whereby an intervention was seen as a legitimate and satisfactory exercise which, although popular, did not tackle the issues it was set up to deal with. The result of this research allowed the researchers to identify a number of ways in which the approach could be developed, or to decide whether different approaches to the problem should be adopted.

Although the approach adopted by McKay and her colleagues was a sophisticated research design, and impractical to replicate on a day-to-day basis in organisations, it serves to demonstrate how important it is for organisations to consider outcomes beyond employee satisfaction with the service. A final issue that organisations need to consider is a more global concern around counselling (or any individually focused intervention) as a technique that addresses individual perspectives and processes often independently of an organisational context.

While counselling helps the individual to cope with the situation they are in, it should not be done in isolation from the job characteristics that might be contributing to the problem. It is important to integrate counselling interventions into organisational processes. The hypothetical danger being proposed is that where counselling is being conducted in an organisational context, but in ignorance of organisational systems and pressures, the result could damage individuals in the long run if it supports them continuing in a job which is harmful to them.

While such a hypothetical question is far removed from the research evidence being considered here, it does highlight two very important issues that have been commented on by several researchers (*eg* Cooper and Cartwright, 1994). These can be summed up as follows:

- The extent to which counsellors need awareness of organisational systems and structures, particularly where clients' presenting problems are work related.
- The extent to which organisations need knowledge of any particular policies or practices that could be contributing to the problems being experienced by employees.

> Evidence from the examples presented here suggests that initial assessment, planning response to identified need, monitoring and evaluation, and feedback to the organisation are all important elements in the process of providing counselling in an organisational context.
>
> Counselling works in its own right: it helps distressed individuals to better understand and cope with the situations they are in. The research evidence available points to the success of counselling in helping people with high levels of psychological distress.
>
> However, research also demonstrates the need for organisations to be very clear about why they are introducing counselling interventions (*ie* what problems they are tackling) and what specifically they aim to achieve in doing so.

3.5.4 Organisational level interventions

Popular models of occupational stress usually identify a range of work areas that can be associated with poor levels of mental health. Job characteristics (stressors) which fall into this area typically include role ambiguity, role conflict, job insecurity, low involvement in decision making, and workload, among others. These factors can be seen as intrinsic to the specific working environment, and as such, it is perhaps surprising that relatively little attention has been focused on organisational change as a way of improving psychological health. It is probable that the medical basis of most models for occupational stress have guided attempts at stress management to focus on the individual symptomotology rather than organisational elements. Increasingly, however, research is focusing on different organisational

Table 3:3 Organisational level stress management strategies

1. Changing organisational characteristics

- Change organisational structure
- Change organisational processes (eg reward systems; selection; training and development systems; socialisation processes; job transfer and job rotation policies; more employee oriented supervision)
- Develop health services

2. Changing role characteristics

- Redefine roles
- Reduce instances of role overload/underload
- Increase participation in decision making
- Reduce role conflict

3. Changing task characteristics

- Design jobs in the light of workers abilities and preferences
- Use workers preferences in selection and placement
- Provide training programmes so that workers can be more skilled
- Individualise the treatment of workers

Source: Newman and Beehr (1979)

approaches and evaluating the impact that they can have on employee well-being as well as organisational performance.

Newman and Beehr (1979) identify a range of organisational level interventions (see Table 3:3). Evidence for the impact of interventions in these different areas remains very limited. Robust research evidence on the efficacy of such interventions is even more scarce than that for stress management aimed at individuals.

There are several studies of worker autonomy which are consistently cited in the literature as examples of well designed and evaluated organisational level interventions, for example, Cox (1993); Burke (1993); and Briner and Reynolds (1996). These studies focus on increasing individual autonomy/control and the impact this has in relation to stress and health. Two examples are described here. The control interventions in these studies involve the introduction of autonomous work groups and increased participation in decision making.

The first study (Wall and Clegg, 1981) increased control over significant aspects of the work process by introducing autonomous work teams. The intervention was introduced in response to assessment by management that workers in a specific department of an organisation were suffering from low morale and motivation, and that productivity was poor. In addition, researchers found low job satisfaction and high levels of psychological distress prior to intervention. Following this initial problem solving assessment, the intervention was implemented. This involved increasing worker control by creating autonomous work groups. Specifically, these groups were given more control over the way they organised rest breaks, paced the work, allocated work and allocated overtime. The researchers found increased group autonomy and task identity, both at six and 18 months following the intervention. They also found that psychological distress was significantly reduced from pre-intervention levels. As a result, they concluded that changing aspects of work can have positive outcomes for employee well-being.

In this study, the process of identifying problems at individual (morale and motivation) and organisational (productivity) levels; generating solutions; implementing strategies (autonomous work groups); and evaluating against objectives (increased autonomy, task identity and reduced psychological distress) is clearly exposed. It demonstrates how carefully assessed and developed interventions can be successful in improving psychological well-being at work.

A second study by Jackson (1983), looked at the effects that increasing participation in decision making had on a range of worker perceptions, including job satisfaction and emotional strain. Following the introduction of a two-day training workshop for supervisors, a regular schedule of more frequent staff meetings was set up. The intervention was evaluated at three and six months and results indicated positive changes in opportunities for influence, reduced role conflict and role ambiguity. Hence, increased involvement in decision making was found to improve role clarity and lessen role conflict which, in turn, were found to be related to increased job satisfaction and reduced emotional strain.

Overall, the research findings from the limited number of studies that are available in this area provide partial evidence for the effectiveness of increasing autonomy in reducing workers' reports of stressors. However, there is also research evidence to show that the results are not always clear cut. Briner and Reynolds (1996), point to other research in this area where the findings are less clear. Such research looking at the impact of introducing autonomous work groups has typically found increased job satisfaction. However, evaluations of these interventions also show that, in some cases, the consequences can be negative as well as positive. For example, Wall *et al.* (1986), in a later study on worker autonomy, also found increased turnover and no change in mental health, work motivation or performance. Cordery *et al.* (1991), who also looked at autonomous work groups, found that in addition to job satisfaction, organisational commitment increased as did turnover and absenteeism. Briner and Reynolds conclude that this indicates that the impact of job redesign is complex and can involve both positive and negative outcomes.

3.6 Summary

The limited research evidence available in this area points to a far more complex picture that that for individual level interventions, and may be an additional reason why relatively little effort has been directed at organisational level interventions to reduce work stress. Despite this, many researchers are now concluding that 'stressor reduction/hazard control are the most promising area for interventions' (Cox, 1993), and that 'job design and organisational change remain the preferred approach to stress management' (Murphy, 1992). However, it is recognised within this that any organisational level intervention requires 'a detailed audit of work stressors and a knowledge of the dynamics of organisational change' (Cox, 1993), and that thorough evaluation of the organisational issues is required prior to the selection of any intervention (Ivancevich and Matteson, 1986).

> Overall, the literature on organisational level stress management suggests that well designed and well evaluated interventions can have some success in reducing the undesirable aspects of some jobs, eg role conflict and role ambiguity, and increasing the positive aspects, eg job satisfaction and organisational commitment. However, the important thing to note is that such changes are by no means uniform. Change can have positive and negative consequences. The very obvious message in this research is the success of tailored interventions to problems identified by thorough and specific assessment and evaluation.

> In other words, the process at an organisational level is far more complex, with a far greater variety of problems, interventions and outcomes than is the case for traditional stress management intervention at the individual level. Despite the more complex nature of designing, implementing and evaluating organisational stress management interventions, it is generally anticipated that work in this area will increase (Burke, 1993) and that it is the most promising area for the future (Cox, 1993).

Identifying that there is a problem with stress in an organisation is only the beginning and doesn't itself help in determining successful management of that situation. The next section goes on to look at how organisations can approach monitoring and identifying problems within the organisation.

4. A Framework for Intervention

This chapter looks at the principles of good practice in stress management that can be extrapolated both from academic research and from the case study organisations participating in the project. A framework for intervention is proposed, supported by examples of good practice in organisational settings.

The eight case study organisations which participated in this research were identified in two ways. Either they had been identified through the academic stress literature as exemplars of successful stress management initiatives, or they were organisations with a keen interest in the area which were currently developing stress management initiatives identified through previous IES research.

As a result, they are organisations operating in different industrial sectors and at different stages in the development of their stress management initiatives. They range from organisations which first started developing stress management initiatives in the early 1980s, to those which are currently developing or reviewing stress management interventions.

4.1 Good practice

Increasingly, researchers and practitioners are recognising the limitations of general, unfocused stress management, and proposing frameworks for interventions in organisations. The point of such frameworks is that they focus in on, and address, specific problems. In doing this, they use processes that are better understood and have a theoretically more sound foundation than stress (*eg* counselling, worker autonomy). This, in turn, brings an understanding of parameters and limitations of intervention, of what can reasonably be expected from specific solutions to specific problems. Creating realistic expectations is also essential in monitoring and evaluating performance and in feeding back into organisational policy.

The examples of good practice from the research literature presented in this report virtually all contained elements of assessment and problem identification as a starting point for intervention. Most interventions had been designed or selected to address the specific problems identified, and virtually all were set up with clear objectives against which outcomes could be measured.

These principles of identifying and targeting specific problems, and setting realistic and measurable objectives, was also prevalent in the approaches taken by the case study organisations. Many of them made the distinction between general concerns about stress and tackling specific workplace problems. The majority of their efforts were clearly in the latter category and, without exception, the essential role of evaluation was a predominant theme. Even in organisations where interventions were too newly established to be judged successful or not, evaluation was planned and was seen as essential to the implementation of a successful stress management intervention.

4.2 An intervention framework

Several researchers and practitioners working in the area of stress management have proposed frameworks for intervention that incorporate the principles of good practice identified here. One such framework proposed by Cox (1993) is that of the control cycle based broadly on the regulations for the Control of Substances Hazardous to Health, 1980, 1990 (COSHH) (see Figure 4:1).

The problem solving, cyclical approach is clearly an attractive one. It provides both a systematic and a proactive approach to dealing with issues in organisations. Its cyclical nature implies continuous improvement in problem solving and problem management. However, Cox's model for intervention or managing mental health at work does have difficulties because it rests on the assumption of clear links between sources of stress, experience of strain, individual and organisational outcomes, and the success of stress management interventions in limiting the consequences.

Figure 4:1 Control Cycle and the Management of Stress

(1) Acceptance that employees are experiencing problems or stress at work.

(2) Analysis of the possibly stressful situation, with the identification of the psychosocial and other hazards involved, the nature of the harm that they might cause and the possible mechanisms by which the hazards, the experience of stress and the harm are related.

(3) Assessment of the risk to health associated with those hazards and the experience of stress.

(4) Design of reasonable and practicable control strategies.

(5) Planning implementation of those strategies.

(6) Monitoring and evaluation of the effects of those strategies, feeding back into a re-appraisal of the whole process.

Source: Cox, 1993

Cox, for example, proposes 'analysis of the possibly stressful situation, with the identification of the psychosocial and other hazards involved, the nature of the harm that they might cause and the possible mechanisms by which the hazards, the experience of stress and the harm are related'. This is based on existing models of stress which assume we can accurately assess links between cause and effect *a priori* and assess risks from specific situations.

To date, the research on stress has been essential in raising mental health as an issue in the workplace. There is broad agreement about aspects of work that are commonly associated with stress, or poor levels of psychological well-being. However, the findings from such studies also indicate that the relationship between work and well-being is a complex one. Often there are other mediating factors. The danger of basing analysis and assessment of risk on the broad concept of stress is that vague diagnosis will result.

One of the key issues emerging from the research reviewed here and found in the case study organisations, was the role of assessment and problem diagnosis. Even so, the approach proposed by Cox provides a very useful framework for understanding the good practice highlighted in this research, and for guiding organisations in implementing stress management initiatives if used in a more focused way.

4.2.1 Five key elements

This research identifies five key areas of good practice which can be seen as a problem solving cycle.

1. **Assessment and diagnosis** — *identification of problems/concerns in the workplace. This needs to go beyond the recognition that there is anecdotal evidence of stress in the workplace: why do organisations think they have a problem with stress? What is the evidence? and what do they mean by stress (what is the specific problem)?*

   Generally speaking, case study organisations tended to use a combination of different pieces of management information and specific exercises to assess and identify potential problems in the workplace.

   In Case Study A, assessment was carried out by an 'employee satisfaction survey'. This helped the organisation to diagnose specific problems in relation to communication. Case Study B used sickness absence and two specific exercises. This enabled them to identify barriers between middle and senior management and career progression issues.

   At Marks & Spencer, a series of 'managing pressure' pilots were undertaken to address staff concerns and assess experience of stress, whereas at Nationwide, absence data is monitored and used to identify pockets of high pressure. Additionally, certain roles are recognised to be potentially stressful (*eg* lone worker roles) and these are then examined in greater detail.

   The Post Office has assessed and diagnosed problems through medical retirement statistics and through feedback from an employee counselling service, which identified stress as one of the main problems that prompted people to seek counselling.

2. **Solution generation** — *what types of actions are appropriate and what are the aims in taking them? What does the organisation want to achieve in tackling the problem? What options for intervention does the organisation have? What would be the goals that the organisation hopes to achieve by intervening?*

   To some extent, the generation of solutions will be guided by the initial analysis and identification of problems. In this research, the case study organisations had initiated a variety of different approaches based on the problems that they had identified. Broadly, these can be seen as initiatives focused on the individual and their organisation. However, an interesting finding is that in no case was a single approach on its own seen as appropriate. Often organisations implemented a number of different approaches, as befitted the issues they had identified.

For example, Marks & Spencer identified three broad areas:

- using performance appraisal and individual development programmes to ensure that individuals have the skills required to fulfil their roles within the organisation
- providing a welfare line and providing good practice on specific issues, such as elder care, to assist employees in dealing with pressure from home, and
- seeking to optimise their health provision to maintain as healthy an organisation as possible.

In addition, at an organisational level, they have introduced four teams into each store. These teams play an important communication role with managers and can take on a problem-solving role within stores.

Rolls-Royce, on the other hand, identified a correlation in certain business areas between time off due to stress and weaker management systems, organisation restructuring and recent industrial relations problems. As a result, their activities focused on increased management awareness, using employee medicals to assess lifestyle factors, and provision of employee assistance services.

At Nestlé, the approach has been far reaching and moved away from perceptions of stress. Occupational health and safety is incorporated into the business strategy, and a broad range of interventions have been set up in a structured way which involves defining and resourcing programmes, setting objectives, communicating effectively to employees, and establishing an ongoing cycle of programme management and review.

3. **Implementation** — *if at all possible, in a way that allows for controlled comparisons. How should the intervention be structured? Over what timescale?*

A striking finding from our case studies was that implementation of stress management initiatives was never viewed as a discrete action, but always as part of a process. In all cases, implementation of programmes was set up in such a way that some form of evaluation and feedback was in place. This is a key principle underlying the good practice identified in the case studies.

Further important factors in determining successful implementation are around the support of top management for the intervention, and the way it is communicated to employees.

Support from senior management was evident in all our case study organisations. The way that communication about stress management took place varied depending on what was appropriate to the organisation and the type of intervention. For example, at Marks & Spencer, there is a programme of 'managing pressure' workshops. What is of note is that all case study organisations had a clear communication strategy in relation to stress at work.

4. **Evaluation** — *consequences of intervention against expectation of positive and negative outcomes. How and when will the intervention be evaluated? Are there pre-determined success criteria?*

All case study organisations placed emphasis on the evaluation of their stress management interventions. Several were still in their infancy, but had set timescales for the completion of initial evaluation work. This could take the form of one-off evaluations, or, depending on the objectives of the intervention, could also contribute to ongoing monitoring and feedback. Those case study organisations with more established interventions used a variety of different techniques for establishing how well they had met their objectives. Often, sickness absence was used in conjunction with other information, eg using standardised questionnaires, feedback from workshops or employee surveys. Other approaches used medical retirement statistics and detailed cost benefit analysis.

5. **Ongoing monitoring and feedback** *into the assessment process. How can assessment findings be integrated with other management structures and policies?*

Ongoing monitoring and feedback played an important role for all case study organisations in several ways. Firstly, in terms of helping them to develop initiatives already in place; secondly, by feeding back to the organisations on potential or actual areas of work which could then be assessed and dealt with in other ways; and thirdly, in providing reassessment of existing issues and feedback on changes that were occurring. This final element of the process was particularly important in helping organisations to become more expert at understanding how specific systems or practices in their organisations were likely to affect the well-being of individuals employed there.

4.3 Conclusion

The framework for intervention proposed here incorporates the many features of good practice identified in the case studies. It has the advantage of being flexible and can be adapted to many different organisational settings. The structure facilitates good practice regardless of whether the problem solving cycle is being applied to individuals or organisations, and regardless of whether the aim of intervention is primary, secondary or tertiary.

Equally, it can be used as a starting point, or as a way of reviewing existing activities and identifying areas where activities could be strengthened or developed.

5. Conclusion and Summary

Organisations today face a difficult dilemma. On the one hand, occupational stress is a very big issue and there has been an unprecedented growth in awareness of work-related stress and psychological well-being over the last few decades. At the same time, they face new or more clearly defined responsibilities in relation to employee mental health.

The start of this report described how the discourse on stress has grown over the last few decades, and discussed some of the reasons why it has remained such a persuasive concept. Part of that appeal lies in its ability to provide a simple but all encompassing analysis of any source of distress in everyday life. On the other hand, what is meant by stress is often poorly defined. This is particularly the case in lay definitions, where the word 'stress' is often used to describe aspects of work or home life; a range of negative feelings or emotions; and (as the work of Pollock shows) stress is often cited as the cause of physical symptoms as diverse as headaches and cardiovascular heart disease.

It is the very popularity of stress that causes many of the difficulties that exist around its definition and conceptualisation. On the one hand, we view it as a normal part of everyday life; on the other, a potential cause of serious illness. 'Part of the problem is that stress is an umbrella term and the causes, context and responses will all vary.' (Cary Cooper, *The Independent*, 8/5/96).

> Because stress has become such a big issue in itself, and such a confused issue in terms of definition, the concept can get in the way of looking at what is actually going on in organisations and at what is, for want of a better term, good stress management practice.

As research knowledge about stress has developed, so general understanding of it has become more consolidated around its use as an organising concept that can explain sequentially-related events. Models of occupational stress distinguish between:

- the sources of stress (or stressors), *ie* different work characteristics which might give rise to problems
- strain, *ie* the individual perceptions and experience, and
- stress outcomes in both the short and long term, and at individual and organisational levels.

Research findings reveal broad concerns about the work characteristics typically associated with poor levels of psychological well-being. However, this research also demonstrates that the extent to which any of these work characteristics will be associated with poor psychological well-being varies according to circumstances, or the context of the specific research setting.

It can be argued that the concept of stress provides a useful framework for organising ideas, but it is only a starting point. 'Stress' does not explain what goes on in organisations and offers only limited advice as to what organisations can do to manage the effects. Calling it stress doesn't really help us to understand or deal with the things that are going on that might affect people's mental health at work.

One of the criticisms of stress management interventions is that they often occur as a discrete activity, *ie* independent of any analysis of problems within an organisation. This has led to a focus on managing the individual consequences of stress, as opposed to understanding the individual within the context of their organisation.

In direct contrast to this, the evidence from both our case study organisations and research suggests that the most successful interventions are those where the organisation's response is based on thorough assessment and diagnosis of specific problems.

Given the diverse range of causes, interventions and outcomes, and the very focused, specific, problem-solving approaches that organisations need to adopt, we have to question just how useful the stress concept is to organisations. 'Stress' in itself is not an analysis. It could be argued that we need to move on from the somewhat vague label of 'stress' to attempt to deal with problems effectively. To know that 50 per cent of workers are suffering from stress does not really help. To know why 50 per cent of workers report feeling stressed is a step forward. It is the *why?* that is crucial.

The problem-solving cycle as a framework for stress management advocated here pulls together the good practice identified in a number of case studies, and in the research literature on stress. It is based on the control cycle approach first proposed by Cox (1993), but suggests a more focused and systemic approach. Much advice on what employers should do about stress is generic advice which can miss out on organisational differences or work-specific factors. One of the advantages of this type of approach is that it is flexible in dealing with a wide range of settings or situations.

It also promotes an approach which encourages a systemic appraisal of issues so that different solutions can be identified and, if appropriate, several strategies can be implemented. This, in turn, reinforces the development of response(s) with clear objectives so that performance can be monitored, and approaches adjusted and developed as necessary.

Using the problem solving cycle advocated here involves dealing with work-based problems; defining the parameters within which you are working, including the scale, scope, antecedents and consequences of that problem; and producing and implementing targeted responses with criteria which allow the process to be evaluated.

CASE STUDIES

Case Study A: Engineering Sector (large employer)

Background

This case study was with an engineering company with 2,600 employees, relying on both civil and defence markets. Recent years have been difficult in their major markets and as a result, the last six years have seen a considerable fall in sales turnover.

This had resulted in cost reductions through rationalising facilities and redundancies. Up to 1993, all redundancies had been made by voluntary severance and natural wastage. In 1993, the first compulsory redundancies took place since 1965. These continued into 1994 and 1995. This process also involved improvements in productivity.

The company had therefore undergone considerable change, which had been unsettling for employees. It was accepted that people do not like change and often found it stressful. They had also found that redundancy rounds were stressful for those retaining their jobs.

Identifying stress

The company analysed sickness absence data on a regular basis. The purpose was to identify those people regularly absent for short periods in order to refer them to occupational health. It was not felt, however, that absence data was a useful indicator of stress in the workplace. This was partly because absence always decreases when redundancies are announced.

It was also felt to be the case that stress-related absence was not usually attributed to stress. GPs will call it something else because employees feel there is still a stigma attached to mental health problems. They fear it will increase the likelihood of redundancy or it may affect promotion prospects.

Despite this, the company was aware that there was a morale and stress problem among staff because of the prevailing environment of cut-backs and change. To better assess what factors were contributing to poor morale, they undertook an employee satisfaction survey. This did not ask whether people were under stress. In a redundancy situation, this was thought to be obvious.

A random selection of 200 employees was taken and the questionnaires were completed anonymously. A number of management workshops with the Managing Director were held to look at the results. This clearly indicated that poor communications in one form or another was a key contributor to low morale and stress. Employees felt ignored and prevented from using their talents in the most effective way.

Organisational intervention

A conclusion from this process was that they needed to look at their management style and approach, and this was felt to fall outside how they ran the business.

From the workshops, they developed a series of organisational initiatives to project a style of ordinary plain good management and regard for people which may well be as effective a way of dealing with stress and reducing its effects as a high profile approach to stress as a company stress programme. These involved personnel processes, training and counselling facilities.

Personnel processes

Investors in People

The first initiative was a commitment to IiP. Although management change was not seen as driven by IiP, the process did raise people issues, of which employee support was one.

Positive annual appraisals

In appraisals, it was realised there should be the recognition of training needs, development needs and judgement of potential.

Most people want to know how they are progressing. The approach had tended to be aimed at what was to be done, not about long-term goals. There was also a move towards more ownership of careers.

Communication

Improving communication was tackled in several ways:

- Weekly departmental communications meetings, with official encouragement that they be 'two-way' communication. It was felt that involvement builds commitment. Involving people before decisions are made makes for better decisions, faster implementation and widespread commitment to the decision.
- Clear communication to all, particularly important during 'stressful' times, such as changes to business operations and/or during periods of redundancy.
- Deliberate seeking of employees' views on how the company is managed and how it could be improved. This includes continued use of employee satisfaction questionnaires. Communication is not the same as telling. It starts with listening and putting things in a way that is relevant to all the people involved.

Valuing individuals

Valuing people for the knowledge and skill they have and the contribution they make: it was felt that the company could only benefit from that if they enable employees to contribute and get all their ideas out in the open.

Teamwork

Teamwork was seen as critical. No individual can have all the right answers. Effective teamwork uses all available talents and enables the company to achieve extraordinary goals. The aim was to focus on improving team-leader skills and team member skills as a priority.

Training

Training was introduced for supervisors and safety representatives by the Occupational Health Department on the recognition of people in 'distress' and the help available.

For individuals, the Training Department offers self-help training through the Learning Resource Centre on the recognition and management of personal stress.

Counselling services

The level of uncertainty and change within the company led management to introduce an external, 24 hour employee assistance programme to provide employees and their families with help on a whole range of problems. These include:

- debt counselling
- relationship difficulties
- alcohol or drug misuse
- loss of confidence
- stress
- bereavement
- workplace reorganisation.

The counselling is not just carried out by telephone but also face-to-face if necessary, through a network of people around the country. Although problems are often not work related, if they affect the individual's performance at work, then it is in the company's interest to help them overcome them.

All this is in addition to the existing informal or formal referral to the Occupational Health Department for assessment, support and possible referral. Referral may be in-house to the Regional Medical Officer; or it may be external, to professional or voluntary groups as appropriate.

Evaluation

Very little has been done on evaluating these practices because they have not been in operation long enough. The employee assistance scheme will be providing feedback in the very near future.

Overall, however, the changes were all regarded as a step forward because they demonstrated that the company cares.

Case Study B: Financial Services Sector (large employer)

This organisation, established at the turn of the century, currently employs 13,000 people. Of these, 9,000 are based in the UK and 3,000 are overseas. 2,000 UK staff are field based, spending the majority of their time away from the office. The organisation's main focus is in insurance and financial services and is provided through five businesses and two supporting functions.

Three businesses offer direct insurance services to a wide variety of customers. These are at the commercial level (*eg* multinational organisations to corner shops), the personal level (*eg* home or car insurance to individual members of the public) and a re-insurance service (for risks — *eg* satellites).

Two further businesses offer financial services (mortgages, PEPs *etc.*) to UK and overseas customers. The two final businesses provide support across the group. The corporate business is at the holding level and deals with investment of capital for the whole organisation. The management services business also provides a range of support services across the whole organisation. These services are quite wide ranging and include IT support, catering contracts, sports facilities *etc.*

Business trends over the last few years have heralded a greater move to telesales. Intermediary roles have been squeezed and there has been increased competition from foreign insurers in the UK sectors of the business. At the same time, the European market is fairly saturated, so it has become harder to generate new business locally. This has contributed to the move towards a global market place.

At the same time, internally, there has been a continual drive for cost cutting and greater efficiency. This has involved delayering of management positions, increased use of IT (reducing some of the lower grade jobs), the removal of duplication in different departments, and the introduction of more flexible working, including people working from home.

Identifying stress

These changes resulted in several hundred jobs going in 1992, and again in 1995. Over the intervening years, there has been some growth in other areas, but in 1996/7 it is anticipated that dozens of jobs at head office will go. It is generally acknowledged in the organisation that people feel insecure, but the actions to date have been necessary for survival.

Centrally, measures of stress can be made through the payroll through stress-related sickness absence and through analysis of doctors' certificates for sick leave. The organisation recognises that sickness absence data is not ideal as an indicator, and it is currently being reviewed. At a local level, sickness is often self-certified, and there is concern about how well that reflects the particular problems that staff are experiencing.

Occupational intervention

The main form of organisational intervention has been through the introduction of a policy on stress and the introduction of a counselling service.

There have recently been two more specific exercises to look at stress within the organisation, both of which have led to organisational level interventions. In 1990, 100 managers were assessed using a standard measure of occupational stress. The results indicated that self-reported stress was higher among middle managers than senior managers. In addition, it indicated barriers between the two groups and a polarisation of middle and senior management positions. As a result, the organisation worked on breaking down the barriers between the two groups and facilitating progression in management positions.

A separate initiative also took place in 1990 to look at stress from working with display screen equipment (DSE). It was found that the typical office met best practice requirements, and that there was a good working environment. The organisation saw the opportunity to develop aspects of job design which included ensuring that work was spread evenly and that individuals had a fair say in their job role.

Responsibilities

Responsibility for managing stress is identified at several levels within the organisation. There is a responsibility for line managers to look out for and monitor signs of stress within their staff, and to deal with such situations in a sympathetic way. The stress policy identifies several potential sources of stress as follows:

- personal characteristics and attitudes
- the job itself
- organisation structure and climate
- the external environment.

Within each of the potential areas of stress identified above, the stress policy goes on to clarify areas of action and support. At the individual level, this is done through the availability of, for example, time management programmes and through medical checks (for more senior personnel). The job itself as a source of stress is addressed primarily through job design and redesign. This is an area which the organisation aims to focus on more in the future, although a number of initiatives have already been introduced. Ergonomic checklists have been introduced to assess all staff working with DSE and for those conducting manual handling operations.

At the organisation level, activity focuses on improving communications (*eg* through notice boards and team briefings), through improving feedback to staff by quality appraisals and performance-related pay. Advice on managing external sources of stress is also given in the stress management policy.

Support mechanisms

Managers have access to a large range of videos on managers' pressure at work, either for personal use or as part of local intervention involving groups of staff.

Since July 1995, the organisation has been operating a confidential, externally based, telephone counselling service. This includes the option for up to half a dozen face-to-face meetings anywhere in the country and/or advice from solicitors, debt counsellors *etc.*

The employee relations unit can, with the staff member's agreement, refer the person to the company medical officer who can supply specific advice to the individual and the company.

The organisation is generally supportive and always aims to continue employment where possible. They have a number of alternatives to support an individual in continuing or returning to work and tailor their activity to the specific situation. Options include: reducing the volume of work, temporarily placing the individual on other duties, reforming work relationships, reducing working hours, job design, and job rotation.

Evaluation

The organisation does not make any estimate as to the costs of occupational stress internally, but if the Health and Safety Executive's national figures are adopted, then the cost of stress would be about £1.9 million per year. The main form of assessment of the scale of any problems is through the centrally held records of sickness absence, this however is currently under review.

As the stress counselling service has only been operating for less than a year, no formal evaluation of the service has yet been completed. Initial indications are that the service has generated a lot of interest and the move has been welcomed by staff. The service is currently monitored in terms of number of calls, whether by managers and staff, the business area, and general nature of the problem. Results of this monitoring are fed back to the organisation, as well as feedback on broad organisational characteristics that are sources of problems for individuals. All feedback to the organisation is totally anonymous to protect the identity of the individuals concerned.

Conclusion

In this organisation, the risk of stress has been of particular concern in relation to specific organisational changes, although other sources of stress are clearly recognised. The approach to stress management is flexible and has a problem-solving aspect to meet individual employee needs. The key elements are:

- Providing a clear company policy on stress at work and making it an acceptable topic within the organisation.
- Access to a counselling service to provide specialist help, if and when required.
- The introduction of a number of specific problem-solving initiatives targeted at parts of the organisation where problems have been identified.
- Clearly stated measures which can be used to moderate the environmental influences in individual circumstances where they could be the source of stress.
- In addition, the organisation is currently reviewing a number of its internal auditing processes (*eg* records of sickness absence) to provide an accurate reflection of staff health.
- Finally, the organisation is developing certain aspects of its stress management strategy (*eg* job design) as it receives more feedback from the initiatives already in place.

Case Study C: Marks and Spencer

M&S is a successful retailer which has been expanding market share in an increasingly competitive retail market. It currently has 283 stores in the UK, and stores and franchise operations worldwide. In addition to retailing it develops, designs, researches and resources products in conjunction with its suppliers.

The long-term strategic position has involved a gradual decentralisation process over the last five years. This has meant delayering of the decision-making process and empowerment of individuals at lower levels within the stores.

This has resulted in large changes of role for people working as sales assistants, for example. Whereas in the old days the sales assistant would have been thought of as 'a shop girl who puts the goods in the bag', nowadays, the role of the sales assistant is varied and complex. The principal features of the sales assistant role are to sell merchandise, and manage and maintain their own department. They serve customers, receive customer feedback and take appropriate action, operate and manage tills, complete stock ordering and exploit assisted stock replenishment (a computerised hand held terminal that tells them how much stock they have left on the shelves and in the warehouse that belongs to them). They complete price checks, have a detailed product knowledge and are expected to know what the top ten lines are on a day-to-day basis. They are individually expected to understand the principles of layout and how that affects sales. So, it is almost as if the role of selling has been combined with that of a more traditional role and M&S has done everything it can within the constraints of a very large organisation to enable people to maximise their abilities and allowed sales assistants to become as responsive as they possibly can be to changing needs.

Identifying stress

There was sufficient anecdotal evidence, and there was enough noise being generated within the organisation about stress, to prompt M&S to start a programme that would help tackle the issue. However, M&S recognised the need for such a programme to also help answer some of the unknown questions, such as how much stress was being experienced by staff. So from the start the 'managing pressure' pilot work had two sets of objectives, both to respond to staff concerns and to assess actual levels of stress within the organisation.

As part of the 'managing pressure' workshop trials, M&S looked at the profiles of a group of staff on a standardised occupational stress measure. This measure allows comparison with norms for an adult UK population. This revealed comparatively lower levels of stress within the organisation. In addition, detailed data from occupational health showed that illness within M&S was no more than for the general population. So these results indicate that the organisation has a healthy workforce. To some extent, this finding was anticipated given the investment in occupational health and the health support programme in M&S.

The results from this assessment have led M&S to the position where they concluded that: yes, stress was an issue and it was a particularly noisy issue that was constantly in the media. However, when they looked for the actual size of the problem within M&S, they found firstly that the problem was manageable; and secondly that, in relative terms, the problem within M&S was small.

A further benefit from the pilot process was the development of a model of how pressure can affect individuals within the organisation. This model provides a framework for the intervention that takes place within M&S.

The M&S model identifies three set sources of pressure. These are work, home and health. All individuals have an ability to cope, based on individual coping skills, which are in turn influenced by their personality, training and individual experience. If coping skills are up to the task of dealing with individual sources of pressure, then there is an enhancement outcome. If, however, ability to cope does not meet the demands placed by pressure, then the result is stress.

M&S emphasises the importance of changing circumstances in this model. The sources of pressure identified in the model are dynamic, and change in their relative significance to individuals over time. There are occasions when similar pressures result in different outcomes. This is a flexible and adaptable design which M&S feels could be applied to any individual in any organisation.

Occupational intervention

The model of pressure developed as a result of the assessment work provides M&S with a framework for looking at where they can organisationally influence.

Pressure from work

Work sources of pressure are dealt with primarily through the line personnel function. Part of their function is to ensure that there is an adequate fit between a person's skills and what the organisation is asking them to do. This is ultimately managed by the personnel team who are responsible for ensuring that people are skilled to do the tasks they are asked to perform. It is monitored through the performance appraisal system and through management and individual development programmes. These programmes operate at every level in the company.

M&S are at the stage of another review of their performance appraisal system. One of the considerations for the organisation is whether to increase the total information available. This would ensure that the organisation as a group can see whether an increased proportion of people are doing better on a year-on-year basis. At the same time, they could also look at their casualty rates to make sure that year-on-year, fewer and fewer people are actually falling victim to mental ill health or stress-related illness.

Pressure from home

There is relatively little that organisations can do about the sources of pressure that come from an individual's home life. However, M&S have a welfare department which is currently addressing some of the issues that could affect the home life of an employee and have just launched a welfare helpline. Another consideration is that as part of an ageing society, it is increasingly likely that working age adults will be involved in the care of parents or elderly relatives. It may be that organisations can get involved in elder care insurance in the same way that they get involved in health care insurance. Alternatively, it could be possible to produce information and guidance on caring for elderly parents which helps to pass on good practice in this area. M&S seeks to identify ways in which the organisation can assist individuals in dealing with the pressure that occurs in their home life.

Pressure from ill health

With regard to the third potential source of pressure — that arising from health, M&S has a long-standing and clear organisational policy in this area. They have had a health service since the 1930s and 'aim to keep people as healthy as when they came into M&S, if not send them out healthier when they eventually retire'. As a result, they are continually looking to optimise use of the group health service to make M&S as healthy an organisation as possible.

The influence of personality on coping skills is organisationally recognised through recruitment and selection procedures. M&S recognises that it needs recruits who are capable of being flexible. They have to be prepared to change, to unlearn, relearn, forget about the past and move on again. The organisation addresses this by seeking evidence of ability to cope with and manage different situations at the selection stage. The latest graduate recruitment material paints a very realistic picture of life in the retail business.

Training needs are linked to performance appraisals. There is an extensive training library and network in M&S. Every store has access to a training manager. Everyone receives training as part of their individual development. Training courses are available in all the areas that help people to cope a little bit better when they are under pressure. Such skills include time management, self presentation, dealing with difficult customers, negotiation skills *etc*. The view within M&S is that if the individual's skill set can be enhanced, then the organisation will improve its performance.

Responsibilities

M&S seeks to place the responsibility for managing stress with the individual and likes individuals to take some responsibility for that management. The health service at M&S sees its role as providing the business with advice on the topic, but ownership staying with the line management.

It is important to recognise, however, that individual responsibility is supported by organisational systems at every level. Personnel teams regionally, and in stores, have an enormous role to play, as do line managers, trainers and the staff health and welfare services. M&S sees this approach as working because their environment is one where they have benchmark evidence that stress is relatively low. Hence, their reaction to the subject is in proportion to the size of the problem, not the size of the issue.

For M&S there are two important conditions attached to this approach. Firstly, they see that it behoves them to continuously check that relatively low levels of stress within the organisation are the case. Secondly, they see the need to continuously review whether there are things they could do to manage pressure at work in a better way.

Support mechanisms

M&S has established a network of focus teams over the last few years. There is a focus team in each store and head office department.

From the initial 'managing pressure' workshops that provided M&S with its information on levels of stress within the organisation, a strategy has been devised to roll out further workshops. The aim is to have the chairpersons from all focus teams attend the workshop in the first half of the current financial year. They will then be able to inform staff and colleagues from first hand experience of the style, content and benefits of this approach. These workshops will be half a day in length. The workshop format will be to present the organisation's model of pressures and emphasise how pressure and stress differ. It will also focus on how people cope, and where individuals can go within the company for help in enhancing their coping skills. The workshops will also look at how individuals can recognise the signs and symptoms of stress in themselves and others, and what to do about it if they do see the signs. This programme will be accompanied by the launch of a personal skills booklet called 'Managing Your Pressure'.

There will also be an element of evaluation built in to the workshops, providing an additional source of information on well-being within the organisation.

One of the uses for this information is to ensure that the organisation recognises any areas where they are behaving differently or having difficulties, so that action can be taken.

To some extent, M&S feels that it needs to undo some of the messages from the 'stress industry', which has said that all stress comes from work and that employers are responsible for the stress.

Evaluation

M&S will be examining the feedback from focus teams as to what they gained from the 'managing pressure' workshops. They will also reassess the information recorded and the actual outcomes from attending the workshops. Measures of stress will be collected via a standardised questionnaire as part of the workshops and all this evidence will then be reviewed to identify the messages that are emerging for the organisation.

M&S also considers that it will eventually need to establish a set of its own norms for comparison purposes rather than use the general population norms. It recognises that it performs well against the general population in terms of a healthy workforce and feels that results based on M&S norms will provide more specific feedback for the organisation.

Conclusion

In this example, an emphasis is placed on the difference between stress and pressure, and on enhancing individuals' ability to deal with pressure regardless of the source. Whilst most emphasis is placed on the individual for stress management, this is within the context of strong organisational systems which support the individual in performing their job. The key element of the M&S approach to managing pressure are as follows:

- assessing the extent to which the organisation can have a positive influence in relation to different sources of pressure
- providing workshops to educate and inform employees about stress and pressure
- empowering individuals to enhance their own portfolio of skills for dealing with pressure
- constantly monitoring and evaluating well-being within the organisation and the way it is managed to identify any improvements that can be made to existing support systems and structures.

Case Study D: Nationwide

The Nationwide provides a variety of financial services. Most recently it has launched Nationwide Direct (a telephone-based mortgage operation, which breaks with traditional organisational structures by using, for example, self-managed work teams and flexible contracting); and Nationwide Life (unit trusts). Both these products represent the culmination of a period of internal change within the organisation. These changes have, in the main, been driven by changes in the financial services sector. They have led to the business becoming more profit driven, and there is far more budget control. Cost income ratios, management costs and cost centres are all new facets of life. There have also been significant internal changes in the sense that everything about the business has become more focused and they have introduced a flatter structure resulting in an increase in communications. All these influences have led to a restatement of what Nationwide is about, what it is there to do, and the critical success factors are now clear. In terms of quality and mission, the Nationwide has focused on three areas:

1. The Nationwide is where I want to work (employees).
2. The Nationwide is where I want to do business (customers).
3. The Nationwide is the best performing financial provider (business community).

There are other business factors influencing staff morale at the present time. The main ones are to do with the organisation's increased market share — staff understand where the Nationwide is in the market place and how it compares with other companies. In addition, the innovative approaches developed with Nationwide Life and Direct have demonstrated its commitment to its mission.

Despite these positive developments, perceived job security remains an issue within the organisation. Those still at Nationwide have experienced colleagues leaving, and the use of fixed-term contracts has become more widespread.

Identifying stress

Stress has been of growing concern within the organisation and has led to the recent formulation of a stress management policy which is published in their personnel manual.

A Guide to Managing Stress has been developed to support the stress management policy and was sent to all employees by the Chief Safety Officer. It was designed to help all employees to understand what they could do to control levels of stress in themselves, and what they could do to help their friends and colleagues.

In addition, information on levels of stress within the organisation is assessed through a variety of different measures. The Nationwide retains an external counsellor who provides counselling to individuals based at the Northampton administrative centre and the Swindon Head Office. The counsellor and human resource consultants hold regular case conferences. Here, information can be fed back to the organisation on an anonymous basis, about the types of problems that are being presented at counselling and whether there are any pockets of stress within the organisation.

Absence data is analysed on the basis of incidence, length and reason. This has revealed that in the worst absence cases where stress is identified as the cause, the organisation is only looking at relatively small patterns of absence. However, once stress has been identified as causing absence in a particular case, the company policy is to contact the individual within a week to assess if there is a work-based problem. Although there is no specific analysis of this data, it contributes to the overall management of stress and an awareness of the extent of stress-related absence.

The Nationwide is also currently identifying areas where they feel that there might be pockets of high pressure within the organisation. This work is currently focused on lone-worker roles where workers are more isolated as they work from home, are not part of a team, and therefore may lack a support mechanism. Nationwide is currently conducting a survey of workers in such roles, through a joint staff association and management questionnaire.

Finally, Nationwide conducts an annual 'Viewpoint' survey on an organisation-wide basis. This survey includes an employee satisfaction index that provides the organisation with regular feedback on the views of its staff.

Occupational intervention

The Nationwide has developed a 'Healthy Lifestyle at Work' programme, which provides a variety of services. These services have developed over several years and in a fairly *ad hoc* way.

Nationwide has currently undertaken a full review of their Healthy Lifestyle at Work programme internally, and has conducted a benchmarking exercise against other organisations. Through this, they have identified that Nationwide has been very proactive in looking at health at work and that their level of provision in this area is well above what is required by law. However, this review has also confirmed that much of the development of services has occurred without any assessment of the extent to which stress may be a problem within the organisation, and in the absence of any evaluation regarding the efficacy of such initiatives.

Currently, Nationwide is working on putting the services that they provide into a context of assessment and evaluation. The prevailing paradigm for managing occupational health is being applied to the management of stress. This process will involve conducting risk assessment and risk management exercises, evaluation and learning. As part of this activity, organisational issues of job design, training, health surveillance and employee support will be examined in terms of the preventative role that they can play in reducing pressure at work.

Responsibilities

Nationwide defines responsibilities for stress management as lying with three distinct groups. These are: managers, employees, and human resources. Each is discussed in turn below.

In line with the general occupational health strategy, managers are responsible for ensuring jobs are designed in such a way as to reduce in-built stressors and recognise the stress caused by management change programmes. They are expected to assist in conducting and communicating the outcome of risk assessments in their area, and for recognising the symptoms of stress. They should take all reasonable steps to ensure that staff are not put under undue pressure at work, or are expected to work long hours for prolonged periods. Finally, managers are expected to measure performance objectively, ensure appropriate feedback is given and where necessary, provide staff with training to enable them to perform effectively.

Where an individual is experiencing stress, managers are expected to show sympathy and provide appropriate support. If they are unsure what action to take, they should, with the agreement of the employee, approach the human resources department for confidential advice.

Employees as a group are encouraged to take all reasonable steps to maintain a healthy lifestyle. They are expected to understand and recognise the symptoms of stress and, if appropriate, identify the main courses. Where stress becomes a problem, employees are encouraged to talk to others in the organisation. This could be a colleague, their manager, their human resource representative or their staff association representative. They are also encouraged to visit their own GP or seek other professional help.

Human resources are responsible for providing advice and support in relation to this policy. This means helping managers in job design and other preventive steps. Assisting managers with return to work programmes for employees who have been absent with a stress-related illness and if appropriate, identifying suitable alternative work for these employees.

Support mechanisms

The 'Healthy Lifestyle at Work' programme comprises two distinct strands. Currently, provision includes a range of services to staff at the Northampton and Swindon offices, such as counselling, chiropody, cholesterol testing, massage and osteopathy. A separate strand to the Healthy Lifestyle programme has been the provision of factsheets, exhibitions and workshops covering such subjects as: stress awareness; taking your habit to work; drinkwise; healthy eating; and having a safe holiday.

In line with findings from its review of this area, Nationwide is at present developing and increasing the role of managers and the human resource department to take a more preventative role in stress management.

As identified in the stress management policy, the human resources department plays an important role in helping managers to deal with workplace stress and in advising on appropriate professional support where required.

Evaluation

At present, it is not possible to identify the scale of the problem within the organisation over and above the information provided by sickness absence data. The absence data reveals relatively small patterns of stress-related absence, with the exception of one or two pockets. Using absence data alone, however, is inherently unreliable and Nationwide has now adopted a policy to provide them with more accurate data, both on the scale of the problem and the efficacy of any intervention.

Conclusion

This is an example of an organisation where the approach now being developed is to treat stress in the same way as other occupational health issues. To that end, the management of stress can be seen as part of a process of:

- risk assessment
- risk management
- evaluation, and
- learning from the exercise.

Case Study E: Nestlé UK

Background

Nestlé UK Ltd has approximately 13,500 employees. They are part of Nestlé SA, which is the world's largest food production business.

Nestlé UK has 28 facilities in the UK of varying sizes, ranging from 4,500 to 11 employees. The majority of sites have around 200 employees. Each site is dedicated to specific products production.

The company has recently undergone considerable change following the acquisition of Rowntree Mackintosh in 1988. Nestlé UK Ltd came into being in 1992, and is now managed with four separate operating divisions.

In 1994, the company started an in-house activity analysis. This reviewed all their activities in terms of what they did, how it was done and by whom. The process was one of restructuring to improve profitability and this inevitably involved change.

Stress at Nestlé

Nestlé UK initially began to look at stress as an occupational health and safety issue five years ago. As a result of these initial examinations, they moved away from the traditional view of stress. Stress is now seen as an outcome of pressure.

Nestlé believe that to be successful in managing pressure, a business must decide whether it wishes to take a reactive, 'first aid' approach and deal with the outcomes and effects upon employees which is defined as stress, or whether they wish to take a proactive, preventative approach, and manage pressure as something which can have both positive and negative effects.

Occupational health and safety generally must be recognised as the responsibility of management, and incorporated within a business strategy, rather than be seen as an optional extra which can be adopted or dropped depending upon the prevailing mood. No programme designed to address an occupational health and safety issue will be effective unless a structured approach is taken. Objectives must be set, and programmes professionally defined and resourced. These must be communicated to all employees, managed and reviewed as a continuing process.

Organisational interventions

The approach adopted by the business has not been specifically designed for handling mental ill health at work. There is no specific policy relating to the subject, but it is utilising and developing sound business and occupational health and safety management strategies.

There are two strands to handling pressure: those involving specific occupational health activities, and those relating to general personnel issues.

Occupational health activities

Senior management medical

The senior management group have the option to have an annual lifestyle evaluation, part of which is a questionnaire designed to evaluate the sources and management of pressure. This includes sections on the sources of pressure, personal life, the degree of control at work, their coping strategies, ability to delegate, time management *etc*. It also analyses their mental and physical health parameters, and job satisfaction. All the results are confidential and no results released without the person's permission; collective, non-personalised results, allow the monitoring of trends.

Staff counselling

There are occupational health and safety departments throughout the business, and all nurses have counselling skills. Employees can self refer or be referred by managers who have identified health issues for which they require expert assistance. They will ask questions about health, lifestyle, alcohol consumption *etc*. Often, these can be used as indicators to draw out what is the real problem, since individuals may not recognise they have difficulties and do not realise there is a cause for it. If the nurses cannot help, they are able to contract someone in or refer the individual on to somewhere else for more expert assistance.

This counselling is important because people will not talk to their manager about not being able to cope. They often feel it will reflect badly on their future careers. For the counselling to be effective, employees must feel confident that they can talk in confidence. There is a huge element of trust and confidence involved which has been built up over a number of years.

The aim of the counselling is to teach people how to manage their current problem so they will have the skills to manage problems they may have in the future.

Counselling the sales force

Sales representatives are under different pressures because, for a large proportion of their time, they work alone and are away from the office. It is therefore more difficult for them to visit an occupational health department. To address their different needs, Nestlé has set up a confidential telephone line for assistance. They are all provided with information about the service on induction.

Health monitoring

The company also offers a voluntary lifestyle evaluation programme on a three year basis for all staff.

Fitness centres

The company provides fitness centres at its two largest sites.

Personnel practices

There are a number of personnel practices the company follows which, although not directly related to stress, will help manage pressure and reduce stress.

Communication

Nestlé has a programme of communication to keep employees aware of the business situation and any developments. A two-way flow of information is also encouraged to allow employees' concerns to be delivered upwards.

Employee empowerment

One area which is thought to relate to pressure or stress is the degree of control that individuals have over their work. At Nestlé, team working is used throughout the organisation. Teams take responsibility for their work and allow people to share ideas. This allows people to manage their own work and pushes authority as low as possible.

Annual appraisal

Another means of avoiding pressure is through a process of annual appraisal and objective setting. Each year, annual objectives and targets of managers are agreed between manager and subordinate. This helps managers to see where needs exist. It supports training needs analysis, careers management and management plans. These are agreed, not imposed, so that an individual can have a large degree of control over what their objectives are over the year. These are also reviewed over the year if their situations change.

Evaluation

To assess the effectiveness of occupational health and HR policies, regular monitoring takes place of absence, accident rates, health screening results, performance against objectives, overtime working, attendances at occupational health departments and counselling attendance.

It was felt, however, that it is very difficult to measure success of the counselling *etc.* so they do not publish the numbers of callers to the counselling services. It was also felt that absence data has too many factors to be useful as an indicator of pressure at a time of change.

More generally, their programmes are thought to be successful because Nestlé has not lost a manager with mental health problems over the last three years. This was felt to be very positive at a time of radical change.

One important outcome of work on pressure and stress is that managers now accepted mental health as an issue and recognise it as a potential problem. This was thought to be a difficult point to reach. Managers are afraid to accept that stress exists because it means accepting that they are also vulnerable.

Case Study F: The Post Office

Background

The Post Office — one of Britain's biggest companies — is a group of businesses which forms the UK's national postal administration. It operates as a public corporation created by statute and accountable to the government. It is headed by a corporate centre which provides strategic direction to all the constituent businesses — Royal Mail, the letters business, Parcelforce, the parcels business, Post Office Counters Ltd, the retail business, and Subscription Services Ltd, which provides a portfolio of specialist services of which the principal is collecting television licence fees for the BBC.

In addition, the Post Office Services Group (located for administrative convenience within Royal Mail) provides a variety of common services across the organisation. These include Occupational Health and Employee Support (previously welfare services).

The Post Office regards its employees as its most valuable asset. It has a long record of concern for their health and well-being and over the past 15 years has gained an enviable reputation for being at the leading edge of well-being promotion. The importance it attaches to maintaining the good health of its staff is shown by its annual investment of £9 million on occupational health and employee support services.

Its initiatives have included programmes to avoid upper limb disorder and back injury, managing your money 'roadshows', the introduction of an ergonomics unit specially focused on workplace design, health 'roadshows', preparation for retirement seminars, the promotion of 'healthy eating' in staff restaurants, health screening and a well woman programme. In 1994, it introduced the largest health/lifestyle screening programme ever undertaken in Britain.

Work such as mail delivery can be physically demanding but The Post Office is, however, most notable for being one of the first organisations to perceive and act upon the growing problem of stress in the workforce.

Stress in the Post Office

The Post Office's forward thinking programme for dealing with stress, which began in the early 1980s, has now become crucial in the 1990s, when stress is fast overtaking cardiovascular malfunction as the biggest health problem facing UK businesses today. However, it should be emphasised that the vast majority of the Post Office's 190,000 employees do not suffer from stress. In fact, the level of stress in the Post Office is comparable to, or in most cases lower than, that in other major UK employers.

The Occupational Health Service (OHS) first looked at the issue of stress in detail during the mid 1980s as a result of a pilot study on counselling within the Post Office. This revealed that among the small percentage of employees attending sessions held by specialist counsellors, stress was seen to be one of the major problems identified in this group. This followed a realisation in the early 1980s that psychiatric and psychological disturbances often associated with stress were the second highest reason for medical retirement, after musculo-skeletal problems. The OHS learnt that stress could be caused by a variety of factors and was very often completely unrelated to work. Some could be related to problems at the workplace (such as pressure of work) but many others could equally well be domestic in origin, relating to finances, marriage, family, *etc.*

Although the OHS had been providing some counselling, there was a growing feeling this was not enough. To address these problems, it set up in 1984 a working party of line managers, personnel staff and health specialists which subsequently recommended that stress counselling should be provided in-house to make it more widely available and in-depth.

Two specialist counsellors were appointed in 1987 and they concentrated initially on two pilot areas: Manchester and Leeds, with two comparable areas selected as controls. As employees, the counsellors became familiar with organisational issues affecting staff and were better able to help than external counsellors. They also helped to formulate and implement Post Office policy and procedures aimed at reducing or eliminating workplace problems.

The first phase of the project was evaluated after 18 months. Already there had been a decrease in sickness absence, authorised special leave and disciplinary measures. The line managers and supervisors of those employees who talked about their counselling reported that the performance of these employees had improved. The initial success of the project could be measured by the numbers of employees contacting the counsellors on the recommendation of others whom the service had already helped. In addition, there were also several requests to help employees from outside the pilot area.

Because the two counsellors were unable to meet the growing demand, they started to develop the counselling skills of other staff in the OHS. They developed a counselling skills programme which was later also offered to welfare and personnel staff.

Another benefit of the pilot programme was that it revealed a need for education about stress. As a result, seminars are run in the workplace as the need arises. These seminars include sessions on how to recognise stress and how to reduce stress by physical and mental activities. They also address some of the workplace problems which cause stress. Time management and assertiveness skills, and a management style which encourages worker participation, are all practised as a means to eliminate workplace causes. Specific skills training can be offered to managers when needed, such as listening and responding skills. One further result of the pilot project was a Post Office decision to devote greater resources to developing the counselling skills of the other staff and to increase education about stress.

Sickness absence is a further indicator used by the Post Office. All sickness absence data are held on computer with grade of job, location, and type of illness. They are used with caution, because sickness absence may not necessarily be an accurate level of stress levels. What is often reported in sick absence is the physical result of stress, not the stress itself, because there is perceived to be a stigma attached to an illness that can be described in any way as 'mental'.

A further review in 1993 and 1994, identified a need for support in this psycho-social area of employee well-being. This led to a change in the emphasis of Employee Support (ES) — formerly known as Welfare Services — away from its hitherto main focus on social issues. As Employee Support, it now embraces psychological aspects of employee well-being and took on greater responsibility for providing support for employees affected by stress, developing joint approaches with the OHS.

Organisational interventions

With about 16 per cent of Post Office employees taking advantage each year of the full range of employee support products — of which stress counselling is just one product on offer — ES needed to establish an efficient and customer-focused process for meeting this demand. Following consultations, it set up a telephone helpline as a central intake point rather than rely on employees attending personally, which could be wasteful and provided only limited access.

This initial contact enables a trained Employee Support Adviser (ESA) to assess the caller's needs and determine whether further legal, financial or social information is required. The ESA can also arrange an appointment for a face-to-face meeting with a local ESA for more detailed assessment of need. These meetings tend to run from 20 minutes to an hour, and are often all that is required to resolve the employee's difficulties.

More specific, in-depth assessments, lasting for 90 minutes or more, are offered where necessary, covering such subjects as bereavement, debt management, harassment, stress, medical retirement, social well-being and substance abuse. The objective of these assessments is to empower people so that they can cope with their own situations, rather than make them dependent on ES. Employees reluctant to engage in a personal meeting are sent self-help packs which cover preparation for retirement, early retirement, debt management, bereavement and probate, trauma and violence at work, and stress.

Counselling and education

After the initial assessment, ES may offer particular employees short-term interventions involving first-line counselling, specifically designed for the Post Office. As previously mentioned, the

Post Office has devoted resources to increasing the counselling skills of its own staff and counselling models developed internally are considered more appropriate for use in the organisation.

Counselling interventions are designed to be completed in four to six sessions. They cover bereavement support, critical incident debriefing, debt management, first-line counselling, harassment support, medical retirement support, social well-being support and substance abuse management.

Employee seminars have been developed to provide some of the tools and knowledge required to help employees resolve their problems and increase their personal skills. They can be provided for individuals or working groups which may need specific training. Seminars fall into three categories: stress education, coping skills, and social education.

In addition, ES provides help for managers to enable them to manage problems themselves rather than rely on 'experts' from elsewhere in the organisation. ES offers advice on how to handle troubled employees without infringing confidentiality, either through written assessments or attending case conferences.

Managers can also take advantage of two training courses. One deals with debriefings, training managers in supporting employees who become victims of violence in the workplace. It covers all aspects of an incident and its aftermath, ranging from how to get people back to work, to liaison with the police. The course value has been demonstrated by a halving of sick absence in one Post Office business whose managers had been given debriefing management — equivalent to recovering the cost in the first year.

The second course — caring for people — provides managers with the means to identify troubled employees and improves their ability to support these employees effectively.

Environmental stress audits

The Post Office place a very high priority on health and safety at the workplace and as part of the corporation's overall aim to minimise stress, ES and OHS collaborate in carrying out, where necessary, environmental stress audits: assessments examining psychological and physical sources of stress within the workplace.

The decision to carry out an assessment is usually triggered by sickness absence data, falls in performance or low staff morale. These assessments are now enabling the Post Office to build up profiles for environmental comparisons with other groups.

Assessments can combine a variety of elements depending on the needs of the client, as follows:

Physical environment

This assessment covers more than just safety checks; It covers lighting, heating, dust, noise, odours, space, lifting and other physical factors. It may, for instance, investigate persistent noise which may not exceed 85 dBA (the level quoted in the Noise at Work Regulations) but could distract an individual working on a task demanding uninterrupted concentration. It may look at the ergonomics of an environment which may not give rise to back injury but could still be very wearing. It may examine the extent to which the environment causes employees to feel hassled, or affected by factors such as cooking smells from a kitchen.

Psychological sources

The assessment combines a questionnaire taking ten minutes to complete, with follow-up interviews with one-tenth of the employees on the site. It covers roles at work, career progression, pay, job design, work pace, work organisation and the social dimension of the job.

Physical condition

This examines employees for coronary health risk, general health, physical fitness, and related factors.

Social well-being

Employees are asked in a questionnaire about their social life, including social aspects of their work. The assessment covers interpersonal relationships, coping skills, harassment, bullying, finances, drinking, gambling, and time management and planning.

Findings from environmental stress audits are presented in a report which includes recommendations for improvements to be implemented during the next 12 months. These can include practical things such as installing extra computer terminals or providing new furniture, or substantial organisational changes including work organisation, job design and selection and training. Specific proposals of this kind are felt to be more effective than detailed psychological rationales.

Evaluation

The Post Office's Employee Support organisation has begun to provide a clear specification for all its services. It is agreeing standards of delivery with all its customers — the Post Office businesses and other departments — and has defined roles, responsibilities and levels of competency required to deliver specified products and services.

Services are monitored by customers using agreed quantitative and qualitative measurements, including sickness absence levels, medical retirements and employee satisfaction, as determined by questionnaires.

The effectiveness of courses is determined by gathering immediate post-course assessments of participants. Assessors also return in six months to determine whether individuals or managers are using what was learnt. After a stress audit, assessors return to the site to confirm the success of changes introduced following the audit; some audits are too recent to re-assess.

Reassessment can also be complicated by the changes that the Post Office is now making to enable it to provide new and improved products and services to customers in response to increasing competition in a rapidly changing marketplace. Such changes make it more difficult to determine precisely what has contributed to improvements.

Despite the success of past initiatives, the Post Office is not resting on its laurels. It is continually searching for further ways of improving the well-being of its employees and their environment.

Case Study G: Rolls-Royce, Derby

Background

Rolls-Royce in Derby, as at other sites in Britain, has experienced difficult market circumstances over recent years. This has been mainly due to the effects of the Gulf War on civil aviation and the end of the Cold War on the defence industry.

As a result, the company has been undergoing major restructuring involving redundancies. This led to an increased concern and awareness about stress management. Stress was likely not only from the concerns about redundancy and the loss of colleagues, but also from increased pressures of work: that is, fewer people doing the same amount of work, against a background of increased personal and national economic uncertainty.

The other stressor in the workplace has been technological change. Many people have worked for Rolls-Royce for many years. Older people find it more difficult to cope with the rate of technological changes which has taken place. This has increased considerably over recent years.

Identifying stress

Between two and three years ago medical reports from the different areas of the business showed an increase in consultations for stress-related problems. This triggered further analysis of absence data *etc.* and the inclusion of a mental health policy in the health, safety and environment manual.

Sickness absence

As part of a small project in Derby, the occupational health department developed a coding system for absences outside the

International Classification of Diseases but which is compatible with it. This also assesses health problems which relate to employees' work.

One year of absence records for Derby were coded using this classification, for all the periods of sickness which had been certificated. This amounted to 50,000 work days off sick out of a total of 77,000. They found that the psychological group of illnesses ranked third, accounting for between 8,000 and 10,000 days off in 1994. When broken down into finer categories, they found that anxiety and depression come out on top. No distinction was made between problems arising from work or from the usual social reasons.

Early retirement figures

The occupational health department had also looked at the ill-health early retirement records across the original Rolls-Royce company (the Aerospace Group and some of Industrial Power Group). This showed that 11 per cent were due to mental ill health out of a total of 200 per year (from a workforce of around 25,000 employees).

Mental health policy

The increasing concern regarding stress led the occupational health department to introduce a mental health policy. This sets out the things that managers should look for to identify problems with stress, alcohol, drugs and mental illness such as changes in behaviour, physical signs and other effects. These are prompts advising managers to seek help from the occupational health department.

Causes of stress at work

The analysis of sickness absence allowed Rolls-Royce to plot the broad categories of work related ill-health by business area. This found certain hot spots for time off due to stress. These three areas tended to be those which:

- were known to have weaker management systems in place
- had undergone considerable restructuring
- had suffered recent industrial relations problems.

It was felt that there is a correlation between the style of management and the problem of stress. This was usually attributable to communications. Areas of stress were those where employees felt a 'them and us' attitude existed.

Organisational intervention

Improved management

Avoiding stress was seen to be about good management practices. It was felt that IiP will work towards improving training, development *etc.* and should improve stress at work.

One aspect of this was employee involvement. This has been increasing in some areas, and it was felt that if more of this culture can be cultivated it will inevitably help any communications problems. In the area of health, safety, and environment this has been very successful.

Management awareness

Rolls-Royce has also gone through the route of raising management awareness to tackling stress. When stress first became an issue, two regional medical officers took the opportunity to give presentations on mental health to the Boards of various Rolls-Royce companies. This covered stress, drug addiction, alcohol and mental health. These four are taken together because there is a lot of common ground between them and it is not always easy to tell to which one the symptoms point.

These seminars have continued throughout Rolls-Royce on a regular basis. Sometimes, as part of the seminar, self-assessment forms are distributed to encourage managers to consider their own health.

In addition, managers have been encouraged to come in and discuss stress with occupational health departments.

Senior managers' medicals

All senior managers and those who travel regularly have regular medicals. This generally also includes a standard lifestyle questionnaire which covers questions about:

- pace of work
- extent of travel
- major life events in the last two years
- five specific questions on sleep, irritability and relaxation.

Completing this questionnaire generally resulted in further discussion with the medical officer, again raising awareness of stress or identifying a problem relating to stress. These took place at regular intervals.

Other medicals

In addition to senior managers, a proportion of other employees have regular medicals for other risks at work, *ie* where health surveillance is necessary. These also involve lifestyle questionnaires.

Employee assistance

In the Derby site, there is an in-house employee assistance programme in the form of an employee help centre. The centre has been operating in its current form for four years. It is staffed by three people trained in counselling but who are under supervision from an outside specialist. They undertake a wide range of work, including counselling, visiting the sick at home, liaison with the occupational health department *etc*.

The main aim was to teach people better coping skills and also to let them know that they are not isolated. The degree of consultation depended on the nature of the problem. In some cases, one-off consultations at work.

Evaluation

The employee help centre monitors the number of visits and consultations provided. In addition, the occupational health department is hoping to continue evaluation of sickness absence data both at Derby and other sites.

Conclusion

Stress at Rolls-Royce was recognised as having the potential to cost a lot of lost time, not only from absenteeism but presenteeism also. It was argued that it made business sense to reduce both.

It was accepted that the company cannot control what happens outside work nor control the business climate. It can, however, control the way it manages people. If people have difficulties, regardless of the cause, and the company can provide help, it will be a benefit because stress impacts on work.

Case Study H: South West Water

South West Water is a provider of water and waste water services. It was privatised in 1989 and operates in a regulated business environment. It currently employs 1,800 people: 500 in the Head Office complex and the rest in a large numbers of sites spread around the region, many staffed by few people. The number of employees has declined in recent years in a series of restructurings and reorganisations.

The new ownership structure, the regulatory regime and the business environment following privatisation have contributed to a climate of continual change, in an industry previously used to a more gradual evolutionary existence.

Since privatisation, the company has revamped its health and safety policy. Line managers are responsible for the health and safety of their employees, supported through policy guidelines, training, and audit services from the company's central health and safety group.

Identifying stress

For a number of years, stress was felt to be an underlying problem affecting a range of employees, but there was no structural approach. In 1991, with the employment for the first time of a health and safety manager, limiting occupational stress was recognised as a business responsibility, and systems were put in place to protect employees.

Occupational intervention

In 1993, the central health and safety group developed a company-wide policy on occupational stress. The policy follows the same lines as existing policies on other recognised risks (*eg* manual handling *etc.*). Occupational stress is therefore treated in the same way as any other occupational health condition.

The policy covers all employees. It is described as a 'first step' in tackling occupational stress (defined as a physical and emotional reaction among individuals to an inability to cope with demands and pressures). The policy acknowledges the company's responsibility under the Management of Health and Safety Regulations to assess the possibilities of occupational stress and begin to seek ways to limit it.

One of the aims of the policy is to raise the awareness of all members of managers within the company to the potential impact of occupational stress upon themselves and their staff, and to take the effects of workplace changes on individuals into account. The implemented policy promoted further local initiatives. For example, a working party in one of the company's divisions was charged with reorganising working practices, taking the way people worked and interacted into account in their deliberations.

Responsibilities

In line with the overall health and safety strategy, line managers are responsible for considering stress among their staff. All line managers have been trained to recognise the symptoms of stress and how to approach it. Managers are expected to make full use of regular workplace meetings with their staff (including formal appraisal sessions) to monitor workloads proactively, and to assess their subordinates' behaviour reactively.

It is recognised that in many instances, the causes of personal stress are not necessarily work related, and employees are made aware of the principles of time management, and the impact of certain personal behaviours. The policy states that employees are expected to co-operate with the company by monitoring their own behaviour and seek help if feeling stressed.

Where a manager finds one of their employees suffering from stress they are expected to discuss the situation with the person and, if the cause is work-related, seek to reorganise their workload or responsibilities accordingly.

Support mechanisms

The personnel department has been given the responsibility of reinforcing the overall framework for stress and control. Individual members of staff may also approach the personnel department independently if they feel under strain.

In addition, two specific support services are provided:

- Individuals can be referred for *stress counselling* to the company occupational medical service.
- Since the introduction of the policy, the company has also introduced a confidential helpline, open to all staff and their families. Thus, someone could telephone in, for example, if they thought their partner was over-working and displayed signs of stress, and also someone could telephone in if they were worried that one of their children was suffering from drug abuse. The move to make this facility available to all members of an employee's immediate family was made in recognition that the majority of causes of stress were related to factors outside work, but affecting health at work and business efficiency.

Evaluation

Systems for evaluating stress data are in infancy and it has been difficult for the company to quantify the extent of the problem or provide any firm evidence of the impact of the policy. However, there has been active co-operation by all managers with the policy, with a number of referrals to the stress counselling service.

Generally, the company feels that stress can be a legitimate condition, affecting some people more than others for a variety of personal and organisational reasons.

Conclusion

In this example, stress is seen as one of a number of occupational health conditions from which staff are potentially at risk. The key elements of the company's approach include:

- bringing stress out into the open and to make it an acceptable problem which the company and individuals can seek to address

- seeing stress as similar to any other occupational health risk and placing the onus on managers to monitor the risks to which their employees are exposed
- developing a specific policy to address occupational stress, within the company's overall health and safety framework
- provide specialist help, in the form of the occupational medical service and the stress helpline, if required.

Bibliography

Bailey J M, Bhagat S (1987), 'Meaning and Measurement of Stressors in the Work Environment: An Evaluation' in Kasl S V and Cooper C L (eds) (1987), *Stress and Health: Issues in Research Methodology*, John Wiley and Sons Ltd

Ballard J (1995), 'If it's worth doing . . . it's worth doing well', *Occupational Health Review*, September/October, Issue 57

Barrowman A, (1995) 'Stress — recognising and managing one of the leading causes of executive absenteeism', from *Conference Papers for Successful Strategies to Reduce Absenteeism*, 12-13 September 1995, Park Lane Hotel, London

Beehr T A, O'Hara K (1987), 'Methodological Designs for the Evaluation of Occupational Stress Interventions' in Kasl S V and Cooper C L (eds) (1987), *Stress and Health: Issues in Research Methodology*, John Wiley and Sons Ltd

Berridge J, Cooper C L, (1993) 'Stress and Coping in US Organisations: The Role of the Employee Assistance Programme', in *Work and Stress*, Vol. 7:1, pp. 89-102

Bradley J R, Sutherland V (1994), 'Stress Management in the Workplace: Taking Employees' Views into Account', *Employee Counselling Today*, Vol. 6:1, pp. 4-9

Braverman M, (1992) 'Case Study No. 17: Reducing stress related trauma in the workplace (United States)', *Conditions of Work Digest*, Vol. 2:2, pp. 257-261

Briner R B (1996), 'Making Occupational Stress Management Interventions Work: The Role of Assessment', *Proceedings of the British Psychological Conference*, 3-5 January

Briner R B, Reynolds S (1993), 'Bad Theory and Bad Practice in Occupational Stress', Internal Memo no. A05, MRC/ESRC Social and Applied Psychology Unit, University of Sheffield

Briner R B, Reynolds S (1996), 'The Costs, Benefits, and Limitations of Organisational Level Stress Interventions', submitted to the *Journal of Organizational Behavior*.

Brown R, Bute S, Ford P (1986), *Social workers at risk: the prevention and management of violence*, British Association of Social Workers/Macmillan Education

Bunce D (1997), 'What factors are associated with the outcomes of individual-focused worksite stress management interventions?', American Psychological Association (forthcoming)

Bunce D, West M A (1996), 'Stress Management and Innovation Interventions at Work', *Human Relations*, Vol. 49:2, pp. 209-231

Burke R J (1993), 'Organisational-level Interventions to Reduce Occupational Stressors' in *Work and Stress*, Vol. 7:1, pp. 77-87

Cahill J (1992), 'Case Study No. 8: Computers and stress reduction in social workers in New Jersey', *Conditions of Work Digest*, Vol. 2:2, pp. 197-203

Callan V J (1993), 'Individual and Organisational Strategies for Coping with Organisational Change', *Work and Stress*, Vol. 7:1, pp. 63-75

Connor P E (1991), 'Managing Organisational Stress', *Business Quarterly*, Summer, pp. 61-67

Cooper C L (1989), 'Stress Counselling in the Workplace: The Post Office Experience', *The Psychologist*, September pp. 384-388

Cooper C L, Cartwright S (1994), 'Healthy Mind, Healthy Organisation — A Proactive Approach to Occupational Stress', in *Human Relations*, Vol. 47:4, pp. 455-471

Cooper C L, Cartwright S (1994), 'Stress Management and Counselling: Stress Management Interventions in the Workplace: Stress Counselling and Stress Audits', *British Journal of Guidance and Counselling*, Vol. 22:1, pp. 65-73

Cooper C L, Marshall J (1976), 'Occupational sources of stress: a review of the literature relating to coronary heart disease and mental ill-health', *Journal of Occupational Psychology*, 49, pp. 11-28

Cordery J L, Mueller W S, Smith L M (1991), 'Attitudinal and behavioural effects of autonomous group working: A longitudinal field study', *Academy of Management Journal*, 34, pp. 464-476

Cox T, Ferguson E (1994), 'Measurement of the Subjective Work Environment', *Work and Stress*, Vol. 8:2, pp. 98-09

Cox T (1993), *Stress Research and Stress Management: Putting Theory to Work*, HSE Contract Research Report No. 61, HMSO

Cox T (1985), *Stress*, Macmillan Publishers Ltd, Hong Kong

Cullen J, Sandberg C G (1987), 'Wellness and stress management programmes — a critical evaluation', *Ergonomics* Vol. 30:2, pp. 287-294

Daniels K (1996), 'Stressed?' in Bilberry J (ed.), *The Effective Manager: Perspectives and Illustrations*, Sage

Daniels K (1997), 'Is the empowered worker always happier? Exploring the relationship between job control and psychological well-being', (forthcoming research paper)

Daniels K (undated) 'Stress and stress management', *B800 course reader/workbook*, Open University

DeFrank R S, Cooper C L (1987), 'Worksite Stress Management Interventions: Their Effectiveness and Conceptualisation', *Journal of Managerial Psychology*, Vol. 2, pp. 4-9

Department of Health (1994), *ABC of Mental Health in the Work Place: A Resource Pack for Employers*, Department of Health November

Dewe P (1994), 'EAPs and Stress Management: From Theory to Practice to Comprehensiveness', *Personnel Review*, Vol. 23:7, pp. 21-32

Dewe P J (1992), 'Applying the Concept of Appraisal to Work Stressors: Some Exploratory Analysis', *Human Relations*, Vol. 45:2, pp. 143-164

Di Martino V (1992), 'Occupational Stress: A Preventative Approach', *Conditions of Work Digest*, Vol. 2:2

Dix A (1994), 'Sick Building Syndrome', *Health Service Journal*, February 3

Dooley D, Rook K, Catalano R (1987), 'Job and non-job stressors and their moderators', *Journal of Occupational Psychology*, 60, pp. 115-132

Duckworth D H (1985), 'Is the "organisational stress" construct a red herring? A reply to Glowinkowski and Cooper', *Bulletin of the BPS*, Vol. 38, pp. 401-404

EAR (undated), *Investing in People: Employee Assistance Programmes and Workplace Counselling Services*, Business Development Department, EAR

Eulbery J R, Weekley J A, Bhagat R S (1988), 'Models of Stress in Organizational Research: A Metatheoretical Perspective', *Human Relations*, Vol. 41:4, pp. 331-350

Fingret A (1994), 'Developing a Company Mental Health Plan', in Cooper C L and Williams S (eds) (1994), *Creating Healthy Work Organisations*, John Wiley and Sons Ltd

Fingret A, Smith A (1995), *Occupational Health: A Practical Guide for Managers*, Routledge

Firth-Cozens J, Hardy G E (1992), 'Occupational Stress, clinical treatments and changes in job perceptions', *Journal of Occupational and Organisational Psychology*, Vol. 65, pp. 81-88

Frese M, Zapf D (1998), 'Methodological Issues in the Study of Work Stress: Objective vs Subjective Work Stress and the Question of Longitudinal Studies', in Cooper L and Payne R (1988), *Causes, Coping and Consequences of Stress at Work*, John Wiley and Sons Ltd

Ganster D C (1991), 'Work Stress and Employee Health', *Journal of Management*, Vol. 17:2, pp. 235-271

Hatchwell P (1995), 'Stress Management and Therapy', *Occupational Health Review*, September/October, Issue 57

Haward L R (1960), 'The subjective meaning of stress', *British Medical Journal*, Vol. 33, pp. 185-194

Health and Safety Executive (1994), 'Occupational Stress: Management and the Law', *Health and Safety Bulletin*, June, No. 222, pp. 11-14

Health and Safety Executive (1994), 'Stress and Health at Work', *Health and Safety Information Bulletin*, No. 220, pp. 9-12

Health and Safety Executive (1995), 'Stress and Common Sense', *Health and Safety Bulletin*, July, No. 235, p. 9

Health and Safety Executive (1995), *Stress at Work: A Guide for Employers*, HSE Books

Heaney C *et al.* (1993), 'Industrial Relations, Worksite Stress Reduction and Employee Well-being: A Participatory Action Research Investigation', *Journal of Organizational Behavior*, Vol. 14, pp. 495-510

Hepworth S (1993), *The Psychologist Counselling Service: its development and present operation*, commissioned by the Opsy Branch, Employment Service, Sheffield

Highley J C, Cooper C L (1993), 'Evaluating Employee Assistance/Counselling Programmes: Practical Problems', *Employee Counselling Today*, Vol. 5:5, pp. 13-18

Highley J C, Cooper C L (1994), 'Evaluating EAPs' *Personnel Review*, Vol. 23:7, pp. 46-59

Highley J C, Cooper C L (1996), 'An evaluation of employee assistance and workplace counselling programmes in British Organisations', *Proceedings of the British Psychological Conference*, 3-5 January

Hodgson J T, Jones J R, Osman J (1993), *Self-reported work related illness*, HSE Research Paper 33, HSE Books

Hollis D, Goodson J (1989), 'Stress: The Legal and Organisational Implications', *Employee Responsibilities and Rights Journal*, Vol. 2:4

Ilgen D R (1990), 'Health Issues at Work: Opportunities for Industrial/Organisational Psychology', *American Psychologist*, Vol. 45:2, pp. 273-283

Industrial Society (1995), 'Managing Best Practice', *Managing Stress*, No. 18, The Industrial Society

International Labour Office (1992), *Conditions of Work Digest: Preventing Stress at Work*, Vol. 11, No. 2, International Labour Office, Geneva

IRS (1990), 'Taking the Strain: Combating Stress in the Post Office and Civil Service', *IRS Employment Trends 567*, September 1994, IRS

Ivancevich J M et al. (1990), 'Worksite Stress Management Interventions', *American Psychologist*, February 1990, Vol. 45:2, pp. 252-261

Ivancewich J M, Matteson M T (1986), 'Organizational level stress management interventions: Review and recommendations', *Journal of Organizational Behavior and Management*, 8, pp. 229-248

Jackson S E (1983), 'Participation in decision making as a strategy for reducing job-related strain', *Journal of Applied Psychology*, 68, pp. 3-19

Jenkins R, Warman D (eds) (1993), *Promoting Mental Health Policies in the Workplace*, HMSO

Jenner J R (1986), 'On the way to stress resistance', *Training and Development Journal*, Vol. 40:5, pp. 112-115

Jex S M, Beehr T A, Roberts C K (1992), 'The Meaning of Occupational Stress Items to Survey Respondents', *Journal of Applied Psychology*, October, Vol. 77:5, pp. 623-628

Kerr J H, Vos M C H (1993), 'Employee fitness programmes, absenteeism, and general well-being', *Work and Stress*, Vol. 7:2, pp. 179-190

Korunka C, Weiss A, Karetta B (1993), 'Effects of New Technologies With Special Regard for the Implementation Process *per se*', *Journal of Organizational Behavior*, April, Vol. 14, pp. 331-348

Kwiatkowski R (1996), 'Counselling psychology from an occupational perspective', in James I and Palmer S (1996), *Professional Therapeutic Titles — Myths and Realities*, British Psychological Society Division of Counselling Psychology, Occasional Paper No. 2, BPS

Landsbergis P A, Vivona-Vaughan E (1995), 'Evaluation of an occupational stress intervention in a public agency', *Journal of Organizational Behavior*, Vol. 6, pp. 29-48

Lazarus R S, Folkman S (1984), *Stress, Appraisal and Coping*, Springer, New York

Leadbetter D (1993), 'Trends in assaults on social work staff: the experience of one Scottish department', *British Journal of Social Work*, Vol. 23:6, pp. 613-628

Lefkoe M (1992), 'Unhealthy Business', *Across the Board*, June 27-31

Litchfield P (1995), 'The value of occupational health services in managing sickness absence', from *Conference Papers for Successful Strategies to Reduce Absenteeism*, 12-13 September 1995, Park Lane Hotel, London

MacErlan N (1992), 'Stress: Take the strain of profits: more businesses are putting counsellors in the workplace', *INS*, 31 May

Mackay C J, Cooper C L (1987), 'Occupational Stress and Health: Some Current Issues', in Cooper C L and Robertson I T (eds) (1987), *International Review of Industrial and Organisational Psychology*, John Wiley and Sons Ltd

Matteson M T, Ivancevich J M (1987), 'Individual Stress Management Interventions: Evaluation of Techniques', *Journal of Management Psychology*, Vol. 2:1, pp. 24-30

McAllister P, Bryan P (1993), 'Employee Counselling Service: Evaluating a service', *Employee Counselling Today*, Vol. 5:2, pp. 4-8

McHugh M, Brennan S (1993), 'Managing Work Stress: a key issue for all organisation members', *Employee Counselling Today*, Vol. 5:1, pp. 16-21

McKay K M, King C, Slawek K, Wedderburn A (1995), 'The effectiveness of an individually tailored health education intervention for 24-hour shiftworkers', Paper submitted to the *International Journal of Environmental and Occupational Health*

Millar B (1994), 'Special report: listen very carefully', *Health Service Journal*, 20 January

Millar B (1994), 'Strain Spotters', *Health Service Journal*, 3 February 1994

Millar D M (1994), 'Gaining control over the work environment', in Cooper C L and William S (eds) (1994), *Creating Healthy Work Organisations*, John Wiley and Sons Ltd

Murphy L R (1984), 'Occupational Stress Management: A Review and Appraisal', *Journal of Occupational Psychology*, Vol. 57, pp. 1-15

Murphy L R (1988), 'Workplace Interventions for Stress Reduction and Prevention', in Cooper C L and Payne R (eds) (1988), *Causes, Coping and Consequences of Stress at Work*, John Wiley and Sons Ltd

Murphy L R, Hurrell J J Jr, Quick J C (1992), 'Work and well-being: Where do we go from here?' in Quick J C, Murphy L R, Hurrell J J Jr (eds), *Stress and Well-Being at Work: Assessments and Interventions for Occupational Mental Health*, American Psychological Association, Washington, DC

Newman J E, Beehr T A (1979), 'Personal and Organizational Strategies for Handling Job Stress: a review of research and opinion', *Personnel Psychology*, 32, 1-43

Newton T, Handy J, Fineman S (1995), '*Managing Stress: Emotion and Power at Work*, Sage Publications

NHS (1995), 'The Management of Stress — Personal or Organisational?', *Trust Network: Human Resource Issues*, No. 5, NHS Executive

Norris D, Kedword C (1990), *Violence Against Social Workers: The Implications for Practice*, Jessica Kingsley Publishers

O'Driscoll M P, Cooper C L (1994), 'Coping with work-related stress: a critique of existing measures and a proposal for an alternative methodology', *Journal of Occupational and Organisational Psychology*, Vol. 67, pp. 343-353

Orlans V (1991), 'Evaluating the Benefits of Employee Assistance Programmes', *Employee Counselling Today*, Vol. 3:4, pp. 27-31

Orlans V (1991), 'Stress and Health in UK Organisations: a trade union case study', *Work and Stress*, Vol. 5:4, pp. 325-329

Palmer S, Dryden W (1994), 'Stress Management and Counselling. Stress Management: Approaches and Interventions', *British Journal of Guidance and Counselling*, Vol. 22:1, pp. 5-12

Paxton R, Axlleby J (1994), 'Is stress your occupation?', *Health Service Journal*, November 10

Pearlin L I, Menaghan E G, Leberman M A, Mullan J T (1981), 'The stress process', *Journal of Health and Social Behaviour*, 22, pp. 337-356

Pollock K (1988), 'On the nature of social stress: Production of a modern mythology', *Social Science and Medicine*, 26, pp. 381-392

Porter R (1996), 'A healthy body is all in the mind', *The Independent*, 7 May

Ramanathan C S (1992), 'EAP's Response to Personal Stress and Productivity: Implications for Occupational Social Work', *Social Work*, Vol. 37:3, May, pp. 234-239

Reynolds S, Briner R (1994), 'Stress Management at Work: with whom, for whom and to what ends?' *British Journal of Guidance and Counselling*, Vol. 22:1, pp. 75-89

Reynolds S, Shapiro D A (1991), 'Stress Reduction in Transition: Conceptual Problems in the Design, Implementation and Evaluation of Worksite Stress Management Interventions', *Human Relations*, Vol. 44: 7, pp. 717-733

Reynolds S, Taylor E, Shapiro D A (1993), 'Session Impact in Stress Management Training', *Journal of Occupational and Organisational Psychology*, Vol. 66, pp. 99-113

Richards D (1994), 'Stress Management and Counselling. Traumatic Stress at Work: a Public Health Model', *British Journal of Guidance and Counselling*, Vol. 22:1, pp. 55-64

Rosch P J, Pelletier K R (1989), 'Designing Worksite Stress Management Intervention Programmes' in Murphy L R and Schoenborn (eds) (1989), *Stress Management in Work Settings*, Praeger

Sadri G, Cooper C L (1990), 'An Evaluation of Stress Counselling at Work', Paper presented at the BPS Occupational Psychology Conference, January 1990

Sastry G (1992), 'Case Study No. 17: Using training to prevent or reduce stress in a coalmining company in India', *Conditions of Work Digest*, Vol. 2.2, pp. 268-275

Savery L K, Wooden M (1994), 'The Relative Influence of Life Events and Hassles on Work Related Injuries: Some Australian Evidence', *Human Relations*, Vol. 47:3, pp. 283-305

Seymour J (1995), 'Counting the Cost', *Nursing Times*, Vol. 91:2, May 31

Shakespeare J (1996), 'Running a Stress Management Workshop', *Training Officer*, Vol. 32: 3, April

Smewing C, Cox T, Kuk G (1994), 'Employee assistance, Organizational health and staff well-being in UK hospitals', BPS Occupational Psychology Conference, 1994

Stainbrook G L, Green L W (1989), 'Measurement and evaluation methods for worksite stress-management programmes', in Murphy L R and Schoenborn T F (eds) (1989), *Stress Management in Work Settings*, Praegar

Stewart A M (1987), 'Coping with stress', in Stewart D (ed) (1987) *Handbook of Management Skills*, Gower

Tehrani N (undated), *Evaluation of Employee Care and Counselling Initiatives*, Internal Report for the Post Office

Tehrani N (undated), *The Development of Employee Support: An Evaluation*, Internal Presentation to the Post Office

Trapp R (1992), 'Cures for stress offer big savings: hypnosis is being used to reduce the pressure that can lead to sickness', *INS*, December 6

Wall T D, Kemp N J, Jackson P R, Clegg C W (1986), 'Outcomes of autonomous workgroups: A long-term field experiment', *Academy of Management Journal*, 29, pp. 280-304